PAT BROWN, MBA

# Financial Literacy For Artists

*"Mastering Money as an Artist—From Side Gigs to Full-Time Success"*

ABRAM 47 BROWN

*First published by AbramBrown47 2025*



*First edition*

*ISBN: 978-1-967737-12-3*

*This book was professionally typeset on Reedsy.*
*Find out more at reedsy.com*

# Contents

# Preface

This book is deeply personal to me. It was inspired by years of conversations with my daughter, Ryan "Madison" Brown—a gifted artist and graduate of the Fashion Institute of Technology (F.I.T.). From the moment I saw her sketches as a child to watching her grow into a creative force, I've always been impressed by the way she sees the world. But beyond the beauty of her art, what I've liked most are our talks about money—those practical, foundational lessons that every creative needs to thrive.

We've talked about how to open a bank account and manage it wisely. We've walked through credit—how to build it, how to protect it, and how to avoid the traps that so many young artists fall into. We've discussed Roth IRAs and why it's smart to start saving early, even with small amounts. And when opportunities come her way, from brand partnerships to licensing deals, we've made it a rule that she checks in with her mom and me before signing any contract. Because artistry and business go hand in hand—and one can't flourish without the other.

This book is built from those conversations. It's a guide not just for artists like my daughter, but for anyone who wants to build a life where creativity and financial confidence go side by side.

Here's how to get the most out of it:

- **You can read it cover to cover**, or jump to chapters that speak to where you are now—whether that's budgeting, pricing your work, navigating taxes, or managing burnout.
- **Each chapter ends with practical steps.** These aren't just ideas—they're actions you can take right away.
- **Use it as a reference.** As your career grows, so will your needs. Keep

this book close. Let it evolve with you.

- **Share what you learn.** Talk to your friends, your partner, your collaborators. Conversations around money can open doors to growth and protect you from costly mistakes.

This isn't just a book. It's a tool. A mentor. A conversation starter. A financial compass built by someone who believes in your talent and wants to see it thrive—on the canvas and in your bank account.

This book is a love letter to artists and a blueprint for abundance. I hope it meets you where you are and helps take you where you're meant to go.

— *Patrick Brown, MBA*

Author of *Financial Literacy for Artists*

Proud father of an artist, Madison Brown

# How to Use This Book

***– Financial Literacy for Artists***

This book was designed with *you*—the creative professional—in mind. Whether you're a full-time artist, a weekend warrior, or just starting to monetize your work, *Financial Literacy for Artists* is your roadmap to building a financially secure and creatively fulfilling life.

Here's how to get the most out of it:

**1. Read It in Order—or Jump Around.**

Each chapter builds on core financial concepts, so you can read it from front to back like a course. But if you're short on time or looking for specific guidance (like how to price your work or open a retirement account), feel free to skip ahead. Each chapter is self-contained, with clear examples, definitions, and takeaways.

**2. Highlight What Resonates.**

If a section hits home—whether it's about budgeting, managing inconsistent income, or saying no to bad clients—highlight it. Dog-ear the pages. Make this book yours. Come back to those key points when you're in the thick of a decision and need clarity.

**3. Use the Action Steps at the End of Each Chapter.**

Theory is great. Action is better. Each chapter closes with simple, specific steps you can take to apply what you've just learned. Think of them as small creative "assignments" to build your financial foundation.

**4. Talk About What You're Learning.**

Financial literacy becomes stronger when it's shared. Talk with your fellow artists, creative friends, or even your accountant. Start the conversations we weren't taught to have growing up. You never know who else is struggling—and who might thank you for bringing it up.

**5. Come Back to It as You Grow.**

Your creative career will evolve. So will your financial goals. What feels like too much information today might be exactly what you need a year from now. Keep this book close. Use it like a mentor in print.

This isn't just a financial manual. It's a creative companion for a life where your talent pays, your vision grows, and your money supports—not sabotages—your dreams.

Welcome to the journey. Let's build your future together.

# About the Author

**– Pat Brown, MBA**

*Author of "Financial Literacy for Artists"*

I'm Pat Brown. My story begins on the football field, where I played Division I football at the University of Kansas in the mid-to-late '90s and had the privilege of serving as a team captain. After college, I took my talents to the CFL, where I played for the Calgary Stampeders. Sports taught me discipline, resilience, and how to lead under pressure—but when it came to money, I was underprepared.

No one ever taught me how to build credit, open an investment account, or plan financially for life beyond the game. I was smart, competitive, and driven—but I didn't have the tools. And I quickly learned that I wasn't alone. Financial literacy was missing for so many of us—especially those of us from communities where money wasn't openly discussed. The shame I felt became fuel for a bigger mission.

That mission led me to earn my MBA and become a licensed financial advisor. Over the last 20+ years, I've helped countless individuals, families, and professionals build stronger financial foundations. Along the way, I created educational platforms like *Financial Literacy for NIL, Financial Literacy for Student-Athletes, Financial Literacy for College Coaches,* and *Financial Literacy for the Culture* to bridge the gap between talent and financial knowledge.

So why a book for artists?

Because now, my daughter Ryan "Madison" Brown is part of this world. She's an artist, a visionary, and a proud graduate of the Fashion Institute of Technology (F.I.T.). I've watched her create beauty with her hands and heart—and we've had countless conversations about credit, contracts, savings, Roth IRAs, and building a sustainable creative life.

This book is for her. And it's for every creative out there trying to turn passion into a career without losing financial peace along the way.

Creativity and money don't have to be at odds. You can be both visionary and financially secure. I've lived it. I've taught it. And now I'm honored to help you build it—one decision, one chapter, one smart move at a time.

# Quick Note..

**Let me be clear right from the jump—I'm not a writer, and I'm definitely not trying to pretend to be one. This book isn't going to follow all the formal rules of grammar, structure, or what some people might call "proper book etiquette." You might catch a typo, a run-on sentence, or something that makes an English teacher cringe. And you know what? That's okay.**

**This isn't about being perfect. It's about being real.**

**I wrote this book because I've got a message that needs to be heard. Too many student-athletes are stepping into a new world of money, deals, and decisions—and they're doing it without the tools they need to succeed. That's why this book exists.**

**So if the wording gets a little rough or the grammar isn't textbook, I hope you'll give me some grace and stay focused on what matters most: the information, the message, and the mission.**

**Thanks for reading—and more importantly, thanks for taking your financial future seriously.**

# Part I: Money and the Artist's Mindset

Artists see the world through a different lens—one filled with imagination, vulnerability, experimentation, and personal truth. Whether you're painting with oil on canvas, composing lyrics in a studio, performing on stage, or capturing light through a camera, your work is an expression of your soul. But that creative lens can sometimes clash with the practical demands of financial life.

Money isn't just math—it's emotional, philosophical, and in many ways, creative. And that's why artists need their own language when it comes to financial literacy. This chapter is dedicated to making money make sense to the artistic brain. We'll use analogies and metaphors from music, theater, photography, dance, sculpture, and filmmaking to explain budgeting, investing, debt, taxes, insurance, and long-term planning. Because when you see money as part of your creative toolbox—not your enemy—it becomes something you can shape, design, and direct with intention.

## *The Emotional Canvas: Understanding Your Financial Beliefs*

Every artist has a unique relationship with their craft. The same is true for money. Some view it as security. Others see it as dirty or corrupt. Some chase it. Others run from it. But like any medium—paint, rhythm, light, movement—money is neutral. It's how you use it that defines its impact.

**Action Step:** Reflect on your money story.

- What did you learn about money growing up?

- Do you associate money with safety, shame, control, or freedom?
- How do your creative values affect your financial decisions?

**Artist Analogy:**

*Just like an actor must understand their character's backstory to play the role honestly, you must understand your own financial narrative before rewriting your future.*

## *Rule of Thumb #1: Create a Budget Like You Build a Set*

A set designer never starts building without a plan. Every element serves a purpose. Your budget should work the same way.

**Think of a budget as your stage design:**

- Fixed expenses = the foundation (rent, utilities, insurance)
- Variable expenses = props (food, transport, materials)
- Savings = the rigging and scaffolding (not visible, but essential)
- Investments = your lighting—intended to enhance the future scene

**Action Step:** Use the 50/30/20 rule to start:

- 50% of income for needs
- 30% for wants
- 20% for savings and debt repayment

**Pros:**

- Gives you clarity and direction
- Prevents overspending

**Cons:**

- May feel restrictive at first
- Requires discipline and review

## *Rule of Thumb #2: Diversify Like a Music Producer*

No good producer relies on one sound. They layer instruments, vocals, and effects to create harmony. Financially, this means not relying on one income stream.

**Diversification = different revenue streams:**

- Performing gigs
- Selling prints or merchandise
- Licensing music or artwork
- Freelance contracts
- Online courses or workshops

**Action Step:** Map out 3–5 potential income sources you could realistically grow.

**Pros:**

- Provides stability when one source dries up
- Builds long-term income potential

**Cons:**

- Takes time and energy to manage multiple streams

**Artist Analogy:**

> *Just as an artist doesn't rely on one exhibition, don't rely on one paycheck.*

## *Rule of Thumb #3: Pay Yourself First Like You Frame Your Best Work*

When you finish a piece of art, you often frame it, sign it, protect it. That's what saving is—paying respect to your effort.

**Paying yourself first = saving before spending.**

- Automatically transfer 10%–20% of income to savings.
- Set up a separate account just for long-term savings.

**Action Step:** Automate savings each month. Even $25/week adds up over time.

**Pros:**

- Builds financial cushion
- Prevents living paycheck to paycheck

**Cons:**

- May require temporarily cutting back on discretionary spending

**Artist Analogy:**

> *A great photographer always keeps a backup copy. So should you—with your money.*

## *Rule of Thumb #4: Think Long-Term Like a Sculptor*

Sculptors chip away day by day, knowing the vision will take time

# Chapter 1: Why Artists Need Financial Literacy: Rewriting the "Starving Artist" Narrative and Building Creative Freedom Through Financial Strength

The phrase "starving artist" has long haunted the creative world—looming over studios, rehearsal halls, and blank pages like an unwelcome ghost. It's a romanticized myth, built on the idea that true art must come from struggle, and that pursuing money somehow cheapens your creativity. But let's be clear: this narrative doesn't empower artists—it imprisons them.

Financial literacy isn't the enemy of creativity. It's the fuel. It's the canvas, the stage, the recording studio. Without financial tools, even the most brilliant work may never leave the sketchbook or hard drive. With financial clarity, artists can create on their own terms—without begging, burning out, or selling out.

This chapter is a call to rewrite the "starving artist" myth. To replace scarcity with strategy. To frame money not as a compromise, but as a collaborator. Using metaphors from every artistic corner—photography, painting, acting, music, design—we'll explore rules of thumb, strategies, and action steps that give artists the power to build financial strength without sacrificing their creative soul.

### *Rule of Thumb #1: Budget Like a Director Plans a Shoot*

No director walks onto set without a storyboard, script, and plan. Your finances deserve the same treatment.

**Action Step:** Build a budget using visual tools—pie charts, apps, or color-coded sheets. Think of each dollar as a character. What's their role? Where are they headed?

**Pros:**

- Helps reduce financial anxiety
- Reveals spending leaks

**Cons:**

- May take time to customize for freelance income

**Analogy:** Your budget is your shot list. If you skip it, the whole production can go off schedule—and off budget.

### *Rule of Thumb #2: Save Like a Dancer Strengthens Their Core*

Dancers know that strength comes from the core. It's invisible but essential. Your emergency fund is the financial core that keeps your practice grounded.

**Action Step:** Set up an automatic transfer to a separate savings account. Aim for 3–6 months of essential expenses.

**Pros:**

- Provides security between gigs
- Reduces stress and decision fatigue

**Cons:**

- Takes discipline
- Easy to dip into without clear boundaries

**Analogy:** A dancer can't leap without balance. You can't take creative risks without financial grounding.

### *Rule of Thumb #3: Diversify Like a Musician Arranges an Album*

An album isn't just one track on repeat. It's a variety of sounds, moods, and styles. Your income should be the same.

**Action Step:** Develop multiple income streams—teaching, licensing, freelance gigs, product sales, grants, or patron platforms.

**Pros:**

- Stabilizes income in unpredictable industries
- Taps into different skills and audiences

**Cons:**

- Requires juggling and organization

**Analogy:** Every song won't be a hit—but a strong album builds a loyal fan base and long-term royalties.

### *Rule of Thumb #4: Manage Debt Like an Editor Cuts a Scene*

Editors cut what doesn't serve the story. Same with your debt. Not all debt is bad—but all debt must be directed with intention.

**Action Step:** List every debt with interest rate, minimum payment, and purpose. Choose either the avalanche method (highest interest first) or snowball method (smallest balance first).

**Pros:**

- Builds momentum and clarity
- Reduces long-term costs

**Cons:**

- Can be emotionally tough if the debt carries shame

**Analogy:** Cut the financial scenes that slow your progress. Keep what moves your story forward.

## *Rule of Thumb #5: Invest Like a Photographer Uses Natural Light*

Photographers don't control the sun—but they learn how to use it. Investing is the same. You don't control the market, but you can position yourself to benefit over time.

**Action Step:** Start with a Roth IRA or SEP IRA if self-employed. Choose low-cost index funds. Set recurring contributions.

**Pros:**

- Builds long-term wealth
- Benefits from compound growth

**Cons:**

- Can be confusing without guidance
- Not instantly gratifying

**Analogy:** Investing is shooting during golden hour. It takes planning—but the payoff is worth the wait.

### *Rule of Thumb #6: Treat Taxes Like a Stage Manager Treats a Cue Sheet*

Taxes are part of the show. Ignore them, and the lights go out. Embrace them, and everything runs smoothly.

**Action Step:** Track all expenses, save 25–30% of freelance income, and make quarterly payments.

**Pros:**

- Avoids surprise bills
- Keeps you in good standing with the IRS

**Cons:**

- Takes effort and recordkeeping

**Analogy:** You wouldn't skip your cues on stage. Don't skip your quarterly filings.

### *Rule of Thumb #7: Plan Your Estate Like a Designer Archives a Collection*

Designers preserve their legacy through catalogs, contracts, and brand management. Your financial and creative legacy needs the same care.

**Action Step:** Write a simple will. Assign a power of attorney. Name beneficiaries on accounts.

**Pros:**

- Ensures your work and money go where you intend
- Protects loved ones and collaborators

**Cons:**

- Emotionally difficult for some
- Requires legal setup

**Analogy:** Your body of work deserves a final exhibit. Don't let it disappear because of paperwork.

### *Rewriting the "Starving Artist" Narrative*

The "starving artist" trope says that poverty is noble. That financial struggle proves your commitment. That you have to suffer to be taken seriously.

It's time to flip the script.

**New narrative:**

- Financial empowerment enhances your art.
- Abundance lets you focus on creativity—not survival.
- Wealth is a tool for freedom, generosity, and impact.

**Action Step:** Replace limiting beliefs with affirmations:

- "I deserve to be paid for my craft."
- "My creativity has value in the market."
- "I can thrive artistically and financially."

**Pros of embracing a new narrative:**

- Increases confidence in pricing and pitching
- Encourages long-term planning

**Cons:**

- May require unlearning and healing past experiences

**Analogy:** You wouldn't keep using a broken brush. Don't keep painting with broken beliefs.

## *Building Creative Freedom Through Financial Strength*

Financial strength doesn't just mean having money. It means having choices. It means saying no to bad deals. Saying yes to rest. Funding your own projects. Walking away from exploitation.

**Good Strategy Moving Forward:**

1. **Build clarity** – Know your numbers, rates, expenses, and goals.
2. **Create consistency** – Pay yourself regularly, no matter the gig size.
3. **Establish systems** – Use contracts, invoicing tools, and financial check-ins.
4. **Practice sustainability** – Prioritize health, rest, and creativity.
5. **Invest in community** – Collaborate, trade knowledge, and uplift each other.

**Artist Analogy:**

> *The best projects are not rushed—they're nurtured. Build your finances the same way.*

## *Final Reflection*

Money doesn't make you an artist. But it can make your artistry sustainable. It gives you the power to say no to work that drains you and yes to work that fulfills you. It allows you to create from vision, not desperation.

Financial literacy is not a betrayal of art. It's an extension of it.

It's time to retire the starving artist myth—and replace it with something worthy of your brilliance.

Let's build creative lives rooted in freedom, not fear.

Let's create with our eyes open and our finances in tune.

Let's make money part of the masterpiece.

# Chapter 2: What Kind of Artist Are You?

*Understanding Your Financial Identity Based on Your Creative Discipline*

Every artist walks a different road. A painter might wrestle with how to price a one-of-a-kind canvas. A dancer might wonder how to make money when their body is their business. A musician might collect gig checks in cash and stream royalties in pennies. An actor could be riding high on one booking and unemployed the next. A photographer juggles weddings, product shoots, and editing hours. A writer dreams of book deals while freelancing for magazines. And a digital artist might be thriving on commissions—until the algorithm shifts.

Despite the differences, there is one universal truth: **every artist must understand their financial identity to build a sustainable career.**

Knowing what kind of artist you are—your medium, revenue model, work cycle, and financial risks—is step one in building a solid money foundation. This chapter is your creative mirror. It's not just about your passion. It's about your patterns, pressure points, and profit potential.

We'll walk through each major artist category and break down:

- Financial strengths and challenges
- Revenue sources
- Rules of thumb
- Pros and cons of each path
- Smart strategies moving forward
- Real-world analogies from the arts

Whether you're a sculptor selling at art fairs, a filmmaker building a YouTube empire, or a graphic designer juggling clients, this chapter is built to help you **own your lane and plan your future.**

## Section 1: Painters and Visual Artists

**Mediums:** Oil, acrylic, watercolor, mixed media, canvas, street art
**Revenue Model:** One-time sales, commissions, licensing, merch, prints

### *Financial Reality*

Being a painter is like being a luxury carmaker. Every piece is custom. Every sale is a one-of-one. Your value is perception-based, and the market is subjective.

**Analogy:** Think of your paintings like limited-edition vinyl records. Rare, valuable, but not scalable without reissues or licensing.

### *Rules of Thumb*

- **Don't price from your feelings.** Price from your materials + time + margin + demand.
- **Create tiers of work.** High-end originals, mid-tier limited prints, low-tier merch.
- **Always digitize your work.** That one painting can live a second life on mugs, prints, and digital downloads.
- **Track the time per piece.** It reveals your true hourly rate.
- **Get a resale royalty clause if possible.** If your art resells, you deserve a cut.

### *Pros*

- High potential for large-ticket items
- Ability to build a recognizable style or brand
- Passive income potential through licensing or prints
- Emotional connection with collectors

### *Cons*

- High income volatility
- Non-scalable unless diversified
- Requires marketing and networking
- Physical materials can be expensive

### *Strategy Moving Forward*

- Build a catalog that ranges in size and price
- Sell originals sparingly—license aggressively
- Use sites like Saatchi Art, Etsy, or your own store
- Invest in a quality scanner or camera to digitize work
- Keep a running archive and pricing history

## Section 2: Photographers

**Mediums:** Weddings, portraits, fashion, events, editorial, commercial, product

**Revenue Model:** Per-shoot fees, licensing, print sales, digital downloads

### *Financial Reality*

Photographers are like chefs: people think they're paying for the meal, but they're paying for the prep, the tools, and the years of learning behind the lens.

**Analogy:** Every photo is a frame from your film. Shoot with the end in mind. Capture for now, plan for forever.

### *Rules of Thumb*

- **Charge for your time and rights.** Your camera doesn't make you money—you do.
- **Build packages that offer scalability.** Mini-shoots, retainer clients, upsells.
- **Have a clear licensing structure.** Personal, commercial, exclusive—it matters.
- **Backup your backups.** Your archive is your legacy.
- **Factor post-production time into pricing.** Editing is labor too.

### *Pros*

- Repeat clients possible
- Flexibility in income streams
- Wide market: weddings to corporate
- Ability to upsell and expand

### *Cons*

- Equipment costs and upgrades
- Long hours of unpaid editing
- Clients often undervalue creative labor
- Risk of burnout if overbooked

### *Strategy Moving Forward*

- Diversify between high-paying commercial clients and passion projects
- Build passive income: prints, presets, digital products
- Streamline workflows using Lightroom/Photoshop automation

- Add retainer clients (content creation for brands, monthly shoots)
- Consider second shooters or assistants to scale

## Section 3: Musicians and Producers

**Mediums:** Live performance, studio recording, streaming, licensing
**Revenue Model:** Ticket sales, royalties, merch, sync placements, teaching

### *Financial Reality*

Being a musician is like being a stock. Some months you're hot, some months you're quiet. And most of your dividends come late—if at all.

**Analogy:** Your songs are seeds. Plant them, water them, and let them stream—royalties are slow but cumulative.

### *Rules of Thumb*

- **Gig money is active. Royalties are passive.** Build both.
- **Own your masters.** If you don't, you're working for someone else's legacy.
- **Merch is your margin.** Don't leave money on the table at shows.
- **Know your splits.** Get publishing rights in writing.
- **Teach, license, and produce to diversify.**

### *Pros*

- Multiple income streams possible
- Strong branding and fan loyalty
- Potential for long-term passive royalties
- Performance + digital gives dual exposure

### *Cons*

- Inconsistent pay
- High competition for placements
- Touring can be physically draining
- Royalties take time to build

### *Strategy Moving Forward*

- Register with a PRO (ASCAP/BMI)
- Upload to all streaming platforms using DistroKid, TuneCore, etc.
- Build direct-to-fan models (Bandcamp, Patreon)
- Pitch for sync placements in film/TV
- Offer lessons, sample packs, or production services

## Section 4: Actors, Performers, and Dancers

**Mediums:** Theater, TV, film, commercials, choreography
**Revenue Model:** Gigs, contracts, union work, teaching

### *Financial Reality*

Being a performer is like being a freelancer in a city where everyone wants the same client. It's part passion, part audition, and part mental toughness.

**Analogy:** Every audition is a job interview without a resume. Your body, voice, and presence are the resume.

### *Rules of Thumb*

- **Budget with the assumption of unemployment.** Always prepare for the off-season.
- **Join a union if possible.** SAG/AFTRA/Equity can offer protections.
- **Record everything—voice reels, video reels, resumes.** Be your own

agency.

- **Train, train, train.** The better you are, the more gigs you get.
- **Use income from gigs to build long-term wealth.**

### *Pros*

- High per-project earning potential
- National exposure leads to future work
- Teaching/choreography as scalable income
- Work can lead to sponsorships or endorsements

### *Cons*

- Extremely competitive and inconsistent
- Physical toll (especially for dancers)
- Pay can be delayed and unpredictable
- Typecasting and lack of opportunity in certain regions

### *Strategy Moving Forward*

- Diversify income through teaching, voice work, and commercials
- Always be training or creating—don't wait for the call
- Build a YouTube or digital presence
- Learn to pitch and submit professionally
- Treat every role like a stepping stone, not a destination

# Chapter 3: Breaking Money Shame and Scarcity Thinking

*From Survival Mode to Strategy: Healing Money Trauma and Rewriting Your Financial Story as an Artist*

Let's begin with truth: Most artists weren't handed a healthy relationship with money—we inherited anxiety, confusion, fear, or avoidance. For many of us, the emotions we carry around money didn't start with us. They were handed down like old paintbrushes, passed through generations, often cracked and covered in rust. But here's the good news: they can be replaced.

This chapter is about **rewriting your financial story**, transforming the internalized shame and scarcity into clarity and confidence. This isn't just about numbers. It's about healing.

You're not bad with money—you're just **underexposed to systems**, **overexposed to survival**, and **craving financial safety** in an unpredictable career. Let's walk through how we shift from reactive to proactive, from confusion to control, and from "starving artist" to strategic creative entrepreneur.

## Section I: Understanding Money Shame

## *What Is Money Shame?*

Money shame is the emotional weight we carry when we feel inadequate, unworthy, or embarrassed about our finances.

Artists carry it in specific ways:

- Not charging enough for your work
- Avoiding your bank account balance
- Feeling guilty for wanting to earn
- Believing success means "selling out"
- Thinking others have it all figured out while you're just guessing

**Analogy for Actors:**

You're mid-scene, unsure of your lines, but the audience is watching. You pretend to know what you're doing. That's what living with money shame feels like—constant performance, internal panic.

**Analogy for Musicians:**

It's like playing out of key but pretending it's jazz. Deep down, you're not improvising—you're uncertain.

**Analogy for Photographers:**

It's shooting blind, without checking the histogram, hoping it's exposed right. That's how most of us handle money—by hoping we "got the shot."

## *Where Does Money Shame Come From?*

**1. Family Scripts**

"If you have money, people will ask for it."

"We're not rich, but we get by."

"People like us don't talk about money."

"If you're doing what you love, that's enough."

**2. Community Expectations**

In artist circles, talking about money can feel taboo. Artists are often celebrated for sacrifice—not stability.

**3. Religious or Moral Beliefs**

Equating wealth with greed or thinking that financial ambition is selfish.

**4. The "Starving Artist" Myth**

The false idea that true art must suffer. That real artists shouldn't care about money.

## Section II: From Scarcity to Strategy

### *What Is Scarcity Thinking?*

Scarcity mindset is the belief that there's never enough:

- "I can't afford that."
- "I'm not making enough to save."
- "There's too much competition."
- "I'll never be stable doing this full-time."

**Analogy for Dancers:**

It's like performing on a stage you think could collapse at any moment. You move, but you're always holding back.

**Analogy for Painters:**

It's painting with only two colors because you're afraid the rest of your paints will run out. You're limiting your creativity out of fear.

### *Strategy vs. Survival: The Shift*

**Survival Mode:**

- You wait until money runs out to act.
- You take whatever job pays—even if it drains your soul.
- You avoid looking at numbers.
- You say "yes" when you should say "pay me."

**Strategic Thinking:**

- You track your finances weekly.
- You build a 3–6 month emergency fund.
- You price your work based on real costs + profit.
- You say "no" to underpaying clients so you can say "yes" to aligned ones.

## Section III: Rules of Thumb for Artists Ready to Break the Cycle

1. **If it feels awkward to charge more, you're probably still undercharging.**
2. **"I can't afford to invest" is often a disguised form of fear. Start small.**
3. **Your worth as an artist is not tied to your income—but your peace often is.**
4. **Making more money doesn't change your habits. Mindset shifts do.**
5. **Financial confidence starts with clarity. Know your numbers. Weekly.**
6. **Budgeting is a form of creative direction for your money.**
7. **Avoiding money doesn't protect you—it weakens your position.**
8. **You are allowed to profit from your art. Always.**

## Section IV: Action Steps to Move Forward

### *Step 1: Name Your Money Beliefs*

Write down the three most common things you heard about money growing up.

Example: "Money doesn't grow on trees," or "Rich people are selfish."

Now ask: **Are these beliefs true? Are they serving you as an artist?**

### *Step 2: Make Money a Weekly Ritual*

Artists thrive on rhythm. Make money part of yours.

- 15 minutes each Monday: review your income and expenses.
- Update your budget or money tracker.
- Set a financial intention: book a client, apply for a grant, sell one print.

### *Step 3: Forgive Yourself*

Shame keeps us stuck. Say this aloud:

> *"I forgive myself for what I didn't know. I am learning. I am growing. I am building."*

### *Step 4: Set a Financial Baseline*

- Know your monthly expenses.
- Know your "minimum viable income" (how much you need to survive).
- Know your "thriving income" (what allows you to create without panic).

### *Step 5: Start Charging Based on Value*

- Time + materials + talent + emotional labor + profit
- Raise your prices slowly and consistently
- Offer tiers (budget, standard, premium) to give options

## Section V: The Pros and Cons of Facing Your Financial Fears

**Pros:**

- Peace of mind
- Confidence in pricing and negotiations

- More time for art, less stress
- Ability to invest, save, and grow
- Breaks generational cycles

**Cons:**

- Emotional discomfort
- Temporary confusion or overwhelm
- Might require unlearning old habits
- Could cause friction in relationships used to you "struggling"

**But the truth?**
**The discomfort of change is better than the pain of staying broke.**

## Section VI: Artist-Specific Analogies and Applications

### *For Photographers*

- Tracking money is like setting ISO, aperture, and shutter speed.
- Ignore one setting, and the shot's blown. Same with finances.

### *For Actors*

- Money habits are like rehearsals.
- You can't wing the show and expect a standing ovation.

### *For Musicians*

- Budgeting is like building a setlist.
- You want balance, energy, and structure—not chaos.

### *For Painters*

- Financial planning is your underpainting.
- It's the structure under the masterpiece.

### *For Designers*

- A design without a grid is chaos.
- Your finances need structure too.

### *For Writers*

- Editing is to writing what reviewing your budget is to spending.
- You make the messy first draft work—then refine.

## Section VII: Redefining Financial Success as an Artist

It's not about how much you make.

It's about how aligned your money is with your values, your vision, and your well-being.

**Ask yourself:**

- Do I feel safe in my finances?
- Can I take a break if I need to?
- Do I have to say yes to everything—or can I choose?
- Am I making decisions from panic or purpose?

If you're not where you want to be, it's okay.

You don't have to build a mansion overnight.

You just have to stop pouring your energy into a leaky tent.

# Chapter 4: Passion vs. Paycheck: Can Art and Money Coexist?

*Understanding Commercial Success vs. Creative Integrity Through the Artist's Lens*

"Do what you love and the money will follow" is the dream. "Sell out and you make money but lose yourself" is the fear. But what if both are too simplistic? What if you don't have to choose between creating meaningful art and building meaningful wealth?

This chapter explores the belief that pursuing money will somehow corrupt your art—and that prioritizing passion must always mean poverty. We'll dig into how artists across disciplines can align their vision with sustainable income, and why it's not a betrayal to want both.

You don't have to be starving to be serious. And you don't have to be soulless to be successful.

**Section I: The Tension Between Art and Commerce**

**1. Where the Conflict Starts**

- Cultural narratives: Starving artist, tortured genius, sellout
- Internal narratives: "If I make money, I'm compromising"
- External pressure: Expectations from your art community or audience

**2. Art as Expression vs. Art as Product**

- Personal exploration vs. public appeal

- Making work that sells vs. work that speaks

**Analogy for Musicians:** Writing a love ballad when what you want is to drop a jazz-funk EP

**Analogy for Actors:** Choosing a commercial gig over a passion indie film

**Analogy for Painters:** Creating pop-art prints instead of deeply personal originals

**3. Why This Isn't a Binary**

- Many artists build two lanes: one for commercial income, one for creative freedom
- The myth of either/or keeps artists poor and divided

## Section II: Rules of Thumb for Balancing Art and Income

1. One for me, one for them: Alternate between personal and marketable work
2. If it doesn't pay in dollars, it must pay in growth or exposure
3. Build "income engines" that fund your passion projects
4. Separate money decisions from identity decisions
5. You are allowed to profit from your passion

## Section III: Action Steps to Align Integrity with Income

1. Define your creative boundaries: What you won't do for a check
2. List your non-negotiables: Values you want your work to reflect
3. Identify 3 revenue streams that don't compromise your voice
4. Create a "passion fund": Use commercial work to bankroll personal projects
5. Schedule "free art days" where money isn't part of the decision

## Section IV: Pros and Cons of Commercial Work

**Pros:**

- Income stability
- Industry exposure
- Portfolio growth
- Leverage for bigger opportunities

**Cons:**

- Creative burnout
- Less personal fulfillment
- Potential audience misalignment
- Risk of being creatively pigeonholed

**Strategy:** Define your ratio. 70% income-generating work, 30% self-funded passion—adjust as needed. This balance evolves with your financial cushion.

**Section V: Artist-Specific Lenses**

**Photographers:** Shooting weddings vs. shooting street documentary. You need both. Let one fund the other.

**Musicians:** Corporate jingles vs. full albums. One pays the bills. One feeds the soul.

**Writers:** Ghostwriting vs. your own poetry collection. Same pen, different purposes.

**Painters:** Gallery commissions vs. protest murals. Both are valid.

**Designers:** Brand work vs. original concepts. Let client work sharpen your creative sword.

**Actors:** Sitcom roles vs. stage work. Visibility from one can boost the credibility of the other.

**Filmmakers:** Editing corporate reels by day, shooting indie shorts by night.

**Dancers:** Choreographing for pop stars vs. performing your own modern pieces.

**Section VI: Building Your Dual Path**

**1. Identify your commercial strengths** (What sells?) **2. Know your creative identity** (What matters?) **3. Design two career tracks that feed each other 4. Protect your passion projects with time, budget, and purpose** **5. Build an audience that supports your full self

**Section VII: Why Both Matter**

- Financial freedom fuels creative freedom
- Making art sustainable makes it last
- Commerce doesn't corrupt—lack of boundaries does
- You can teach future artists how to earn without selling out

**Conclusion: You Can Be Both**

You can be a visionary and still charge full price. You can be soulful and still have a savings account. You can be true to your art while building a life that supports it.

Art and money can coexist. Integrity and income are not enemies. You don't have to choose. You have to lead.

# Chapter 5: Shifting from Artist to Creative Entrepreneur

*Why This Mindset Matters in Today's Economy*

In the past, artists waited to be discovered. Today, artists build themselves. The difference? Mindset.

Shifting from artist to creative entrepreneur doesn't mean abandoning your art for money. It means building a system that allows your art to thrive without sacrificing your health, security, or potential. It's the bridge from burnout to balance, from scattered gigs to sustainable growth.

In today's economy, artists who survive know how to navigate both art and infrastructure. Your creative work is the engine. But the business side? That's the wheels, the map, and the gas.

This chapter breaks down how to shift into a creative entrepreneur mindset, what systems and strategies you need, and how to own your art *and* your income.

**Section I: What It Means to Be a Creative Entrepreneur**

A creative entrepreneur is someone who treats their creativity as both a passion and a profession. You make art—but you also:

- Build systems around your workflow
- Understand your finances
- Create multiple income streams
- Own your audience or customer relationship
- Set goals and measure progress

**Analogy: Musicians and Recording Studios** You can be the talent *and* the producer. The studio doesn't limit you—it gives you control.

**Analogy: Photographers and Portfolios** You don't just take great photos. You build packages, manage clients, and deliver polished results.

**Section II: The Mindset Shift From Artist to Entrepreneur**

1. ***From Waiting to Acting*** Stop waiting to be "found" by a gallery, publisher, or agent. Start pitching, launching, and promoting yourself.
2. ***From Projects to Systems*** Don't just chase the next gig. Build repeatable processes.
3. ***From Chaos to Structure*** Creativity thrives in containers. Boundaries create bandwidth.
4. ***From Starving to Scaling*** You're not a burden for wanting more. You're a builder.

**Analogy: Dancers and Rehearsal Schedules** You don't "kill creativity" by blocking out your time—you *elevate* it.

**Section III: Rules of Thumb for Creative Entrepreneurs**

1. 80% of your income should come from 20% of your most aligned efforts (Pareto Principle)
2. Treat your art like an asset, not just an output
3. Don't scale chaos—build systems first
4. Diversify income but unify your brand
5. Focus beats hustle
6. Separate passion from pricing
7. Every artist needs a marketing plan
8. Visibility is currency—spend it wisely
9. Automate what you repeat
10. Ownership is everything (IP, audience, content)

**Section IV: Action Steps to Shift Into Entrepreneurship**

1. **Define Your Creative Offer Stack** What do you offer? Break it down by tiers:

- Free (social content, podcast, newsletter)
- Low ($15 merch, $20 digital prints)
- Mid ($250 photoshoots, $300 commissions)
- High ($5,000 murals, $10,000 brand contracts)

1. **Create a Business Model Map** Write out all the ways you can earn. Keep your top 3. Build systems around them.
2. **Build Your Entrepreneur Calendar**

- Monday = Marketing
- Tuesday = Client work
- Wednesday = Strategy
- Thursday = Outreach
- Friday = Admin and rest

1. **Set Revenue Goals Like a CEO** Start with what you need to live. Add 30% for business expenses. Add 20% for taxes.
2. **Create a Digital Home Base** Don't rely solely on social media. Build a website, newsletter list, or storefront you own.

## Section V: Pros and Cons of Becoming a Creative Entrepreneur

**Pros:**

- Financial sustainability
- More control over your time
- Scalable systems
- Ability to say "no" to misaligned work
- Legacy and asset building

**Cons:**

- Upfront learning curve
- Requires discipline
- You wear multiple hats
- Can feel overwhelming without support

**Strategy Moving Forward:**

- Start small. You don't need an LLC or team to think like a CEO.
- Identify where you're leaking time and money.
- Build slow, but build well.
- Surround yourself with artist-entrepreneurs. Learn from them.

**Section VI: Artist Analogies That Make This Real**

**Writers:** You already know how to structure a story. Now, structure your business.

**Actors:** You prepare headshots, reels, resumes. That's branding.

**Designers:** Systems are your software. Build your brand like a UI/UX experience.

**Musicians:** Treat your albums like product launches.

**Painters:** Your collections are product lines. Your shows are campaigns.

**Filmmakers:** Run your studio, not just your scene. Think beyond the lens.

**Dancers:** Your body is your tool. Your brand is your vehicle. Choreograph both.

**Section VII: The Long Game: Why This Matters Now**

- Algorithms change. Ownership doesn't.
- Economic uncertainty requires creative security.
- Scaling gives you space to rest.
- Building infrastructure lets you say "yes" from a place of choice, not fear.

**You are not selling out by building a business. You are buying in to**

**your long-term freedom.**

**Conclusion: The Artist and the Architect**

You are the artist. But you're also the architect of your career.

Creative entrepreneurship isn't just about chasing money. It's about creating a container for your gift. It's about turning bursts of brilliance into a sustainable legacy. It's about owning your art, your time, and your impact.

You don't have to choose between creativity and control. You get to have both.

# Chapter 6: What Financial Literacy Really Means (For Artists Like You)

*Using Artistic Analogies to Understand Money, Wealth, and Strategic Growth*

Financial literacy isn't about being good at math. It's about learning the language of freedom.

As an artist, you already know how to learn new tools, blend abstract concepts with intuition, and trust your process. That's exactly what financial literacy is. It's learning the craft of managing your money with intention so your creativity doesn't just survive—it flourishes.

In this chapter, we'll walk through the building blocks of financial literacy using creative analogies and discipline-specific metaphors—so whether you paint, shoot, dance, act, write, design, or compose, you'll see yourself in the lessons.

**Section I: The Elements of Financial Literacy**

Just like artists have foundational skills (composition, rhythm, contrast, staging), financial literacy has its own core pillars:

1. **Budgeting** – Your creative plan for where money goes
2. **Saving** – Preparing for the next project or dry season
3. **Credit** – Your reputation in the business of money
4. **Debt** – Borrowing tools that can help or hurt
5. **Investing** – Growing what you already earned
6. **Insurance** – Protecting your creative assets

7. **Taxes** – Navigating what you owe and how to stay ready
8. **Entrepreneurship** – Treating your art like a business

**Section II: Artist Analogies That Make Finance Click**

**1. Budgeting = Your Creative Schedule**

*For dancers and actors:* Budgeting is like setting rehearsal blocks—you don't choreograph blindly; you schedule what happens, when. Money deserves the same structure.

*For writers:* Just like outlining your chapters, budgeting helps you plan your story. Without it, you drift.

*Rule of Thumb:* Budget based on reality, not idealism. Don't plan a musical with the budget of a short film.

**2. Saving = Backup Equipment**

*For photographers:* You always carry extra batteries, memory cards, and lenses. Why? Because stuff happens. Your emergency fund is your creative battery pack.

*Action Step:* Aim for 3–6 months of living expenses in a separate, easy-access savings account.

**3. Credit = Your Artistic Resume**

*For actors:* Casting directors don't know you. They check your reel, your resume, your references. Lenders do the same with credit scores.

*For visual artists:* If a gallery considers representing you, they want a track record. Credit builds yours in the financial world.

*Rule of Thumb:* Use credit like paint—build layers, but don't go heavy in one stroke. Pay on time, keep balances low.

**4. Debt = A Business Loan or a Broken Contract**

*For musicians:* Borrowing can fund your studio time—but if you don't read the fine print, it'll own your masters. Same with financial debt.

*Pros:* Can accelerate growth (student loans, gear)

*Cons:* Can cripple cash flow if unmanaged

*Strategy:* Use debt with a return on investment mindset. Don't use credit for short-term dopamine.

**5. Investing = Passive Revenue Streams**

*For designers:* You make a logo once—it earns for years. Investing is similar. Your money goes to work so you can rest, create, or scale.

*For writers:* Royalties and stocks work the same. Get paid long after the draft is done.

*Rule of Thumb:* Start investing early, consistently, and simply. Index funds. Roth IRAs. Don't chase shiny stocks.

**6. Insurance = Preservation of Your Tools and Talent**

*For sculptors:* If your studio floods, what happens? For dancers: if you get injured? For filmmakers: your equipment gets stolen? Insurance isn't fear—it's foresight.

*Action Step:* Start with liability, renters/home, health, and gear insurance.

**7. Taxes = Grant Reporting and Royalty Splits**

*For everyone:* If you've ever split revenue from a group project, tracked receipts for a grant, or paid fees to a platform—you're halfway there. Taxes are your legal and financial version of this.

*Rule of Thumb:* Save 25–30% of freelance income for taxes. Use a separate account.

**8. Entrepreneurship = Branding, Planning, Systems**

*For all disciplines:* When you go from artist to entrepreneur, you get to shape how you're seen, how you earn, and how you grow.

*Rule of Thumb:* Treat yourself like a client. Schedule CEO days. Build systems. Document processes.

**Section III: Pros and Cons of Becoming Financially Literate**

**Pros:**

- You feel less anxious, more confident
- You make better decisions under pressure
- You can grow your income intentionally
- You protect your art and your future

**Cons:**

- Takes time to unlearn old habits

- Can feel overwhelming at first
- Requires consistency

**Strategy Moving Forward:**

- Commit to learning just one new thing a week
- Keep financial notes like you would a sketchbook or journal
- Use money as a medium: shape it, direct it, color it with intention

## Section IV: Action Steps for Artists Ready to Master Their Money

1. **Open 3 accounts:** Spending, savings, tax
2. **Track every dollar:** Use a simple app or spreadsheet
3. **Set monthly financial goals:** Income, expenses, savings targets
4. **Start a money ritual:** Weekly money check-ins (30 min max)
5. **Get support:** Find a money mentor, community, or course

## Conclusion: Money as a Medium

Money isn't separate from your creative life. It's the canvas you paint your dreams on. It's the equipment that records your music. It's the space that hosts your exhibit. It's the stability that allows your imagination to fly.

Financial literacy is not about restriction. It's about liberation.

You already have what it takes. You're an artist. You know how to learn new forms, find your voice, and build beauty from chaos.

Now do it with your money.

*You are your most valuable asset. Take care of your craft—and your cash.*

# Part II: Building Financial Foundations

*Laying the Groundwork for a Sustainable Creative Life*

As an artist, you understand that before the painting, there's a primed canvas. Before the dance, there's the stretch. Before the solo, there's the warm-up. Financial stability works the same way. You can't improvise your way to peace of mind. You need foundations.

This section is about giving your creativity something to stand on. We'll cover the essentials every artist needs to build a stable, flexible, and supportive financial foundation—even if your income is inconsistent, your gigs unpredictable, and your calendar chaotic.

**Section I: Budgeting for Artists - Making Money Flow Like Music**

*Analogy (Musicians):* Budgeting is your rhythm section. If your money isn't keeping time, the rest of your financial song will fall apart.

***Rule of Thumb:*** Spend 50% on needs, 30% on wants, and save/invest 20%. Adjust for your creative cycle.

***Action Steps:***

1. Track every dollar for 30 days.
2. Build a simple monthly budget using a spreadsheet or app.
3. Create categories unique to your practice (studio rental, gear, printing, etc.)

***Strategy:*** Budget weekly, not monthly, if your income is irregular. Plan your spending in 7-day bursts.

**Section II: Emergency Funds - Your Financial Safety Net**

*Analogy (Actors):* Gigs come and go. Your fund is your understudy. It steps in when life misses its cue.

***Rule of Thumb:*** Save 3–6 months of living expenses.

***Action Steps:***

1. Open a separate high-yield savings account.
2. Name it something empowering: "Freedom Fund."
3. Start with $500, then build.

***Pros:*** Reduces panic, protects your art during slow seasons. ***Cons:*** Takes time to build.

***Strategy:*** Auto-transfer a small amount weekly—even $10. Consistency beats size.

**Section III: Understanding Variable Income - Mastering the Roller-coaster**

*Analogy (Painters):* You sell a big canvas today. Nothing for three weeks. Welcome to the creative economy.

***Rule of Thumb:*** Base your budget on your LOWEST month, not your best.

***Action Steps:***

1. Review last 12 months of income.
2. Find the average and the lowest.
3. Budget using the lowest.

***Strategy:*** Funnel extra income into savings, taxes, and investments the moment it comes in.

**Section IV: Taxes for Creatives - Don't Let Uncle Sam Surprise You**

*Analogy (Photographers):* You wouldn't shoot a wedding without a timeline. Taxes are your financial schedule.

***Rule of Thumb:*** Set aside 25–30% of freelance or gig income for taxes.

***Action Steps:***

1. Open a "Tax Savings" account.
2. Use a bookkeeping tool or spreadsheet to track income and expenses.
3. Pay estimated taxes quarterly.

***Pros:*** No surprise tax bills. More credibility as a business. ***Cons:*** Requires consistent record-keeping.

***Strategy:*** Work with a tax pro who understands the arts.

**Section V: Business Accounts - Separating Personal from Professional**

*Analogy (Designers):* You don't use the same file for drafts and finals. Keep your business money separate.

***Rule of Thumb:*** Always use a dedicated business account for all income and expenses.

***Action Steps:***

1. Open a free or low-fee business checking account.
2. Deposit all payments there.
3. Pay yourself from that account like a paycheck.

***Strategy:*** Link your payment platforms (PayPal, Stripe, etc.) to your business account.

**Section VI: Paying Yourself - Treating Your Art Like a Job**

*Analogy (Filmmakers):* Even indie films pay the director. Pay yourself like the professional you are.

***Rule of Thumb:*** Choose a "payday" each week or month and transfer a set amount to your personal account.

***Action Steps:***

1. Calculate your minimum monthly needs.
2. Transfer that amount from your business to personal account.
3. Leave extra for taxes and growth.

***Strategy:*** This builds consistency and separates spending from income spikes.

**Section VII: Intro to Credit - Building Trust in the Money World**

*Analogy (Writers):* Credit is your reputation. A strong profile opens doors; a weak one gets you passed over.

***Rule of Thumb:*** Keep your credit utilization below 30% and always pay on time.

***Action Steps:***

1. Get a credit card with no annual fee.
2. Use it monthly for small purchases.
3. Pay it off in full.

***Pros:*** Better rates, easier loan access, builds trust. ***Cons:*** Risk of debt if mismanaged.

***Strategy:*** Use credit to build history, not to buy what you can't afford.

**Section VIII: Starting to Save - Building Creative Breathing Room**

*Analogy (Dancers):* Saving is stretching before performance. It keeps you from snapping later.

***Rule of Thumb:*** Start with 10% of your income.

***Action Steps:***

1. Automate savings into a separate account.
2. Label each goal: equipment, travel, cushion, etc.
3. Celebrate milestones—$100, $1,000, $5,000.

***Strategy:*** Create short-term and long-term savings goals. Visualize what you're working toward.

**Section IX: Financial Tools for Artists**

*Apps and platforms:*

- Budgeting: YNAB, Mint, EveryDollar
- Invoicing: Wave, QuickBooks Self-Employed
- Taxes: Keeper, H&R Block Self-Employed

- Banking: Novo, Bluevine, local credit unions

***Action Step:*** Choose one new tool this week and commit to trying it for 30 days.

### Section X: Financial Boundaries - Protecting Your Energy and Your Earnings

*Analogy (Musicians):* You don't play for exposure. You play for value. Set your financial tempo.

***Rule of Thumb:*** If it drains your creativity and doesn't pay, it must either go or be renegotiated.

***Action Steps:***

1. Write a rate card.
2. Have contract templates ready.
3. Say no when it's a "maybe."

***Strategy:*** Start small with boundaries—price minimums, deposit requirements, payment timelines.

### Conclusion: Foundations Are the Frame for Your Freedom

Financial foundations don't restrict your creativity. They protect it. They give you space to think, room to breathe, and resources to grow.

When you budget, you give your money a mission. When you save, you buy yourself time. When you separate business from personal, you elevate your professionalism. When you build your foundation, your art finally has the support to thrive.

Start now. Start messy. Start where you are.

But start.

# Chapter 7: Budgeting for Inconsistent Income

*Planning for Feast-or-Famine Cycles and Mastering Cash Flow as a Creative Freelancer*

If you're an artist, freelancer, or creative entrepreneur, you already know this truth: your income doesn't arrive like a predictable paycheck. It arrives like waves. Sometimes fast and furious. Sometimes flat and silent.

Budgeting with irregular income doesn't mean giving up control—it means learning how to **ride the waves without wiping out**. This chapter will teach you how to budget when your income is unpredictable, using practical strategies and artistic analogies you'll actually relate to.

We'll explore:

- How to create stability in an unstable income world
- Why monthly budgets often fail freelancers
- How to master cash flow instead of feeling at its mercy
- Tools, strategies, and mindsets that work for artists

**Section I: Feast and Famine—Why Creatives Struggle with Budgeting**

*Analogy (Musicians):* Think of your income like touring. Some months, you're playing festivals and headlining shows. Others, you're in the studio earning nothing—but still working.

The problem? Most budgets are designed for salaried people. They assume income is consistent and steady. For us, income is **project-based, seasonal, gig-based, or royalty-driven**.

**Common Budgeting Problems Artists Face:**

- Creating a monthly budget, then blowing it every month
- Overspending during feast seasons
- Panic mode during famine seasons
- Using credit cards as floatation devices

***Rule of Thumb:*** Never build a budget based on your best month. Build it based on your worst.

**Section II: The Rolling Average Method**

*Analogy (Photographers):* Think of your budget like adjusting exposure for changing light. You don't set it and forget it—you average it over time.

**How It Works:**

1. Track your income for the past 6–12 months
2. Add it all up and divide by number of months
3. Use that average as your "base income"

***Pros:***

- Reduces panic when you earn less
- Smooths out feast/famine cycles

***Cons:***

- May feel restrictive when you're earning more

***Action Step:*** Create a spreadsheet and calculate your rolling average today.

**Section III: The Two-Account System**

*Analogy (Actors):* One account is your agent—the other is your producer. One handles payouts, the other manages the budget.

1. **Income Account**: Where all payments land
2. **Operating Budget Account**: Where you pay yourself a "salary"

**Strategy:**

- Every time you get paid, put 100% in Income Account
- Transfer your average monthly "salary" to your Operating Account
- Leave the rest for savings, taxes, and slow months

***Rule of Thumb:*** Pay yourself the same amount on the same day every month (even if you're the boss).

**Section IV: The 4-Bucket Budget**

*Analogy (Painters):* Budget like you mix paint—in layers, with intention. Think of each dollar as a pigment. Every color (bucket) has a purpose.

**Buckets:**

1. **Living Essentials (50%)**: Rent, groceries, insurance
2. **Creative Tools (20%)**: Software, equipment, subscriptions
3. **Freedom Fund (20%)**: Emergency savings, rest periods
4. **Growth (10%)**: Classes, coaching, travel, portfolio upgrades

**Custom Bucket Ideas:**

- "Studio Days"
- "Break the Burnout Fund"
- "Festival Submission Fees"

***Action Step:*** Create your custom buckets in your budget tool of choice.

**Section V: Creating a Minimum Viable Income (MVI)**

*Analogy (Designers):* This is your "grid system." It's the structure everything builds on.

Your MVI is the **bare minimum amount you need to live and work**, without extras or extras panic.

**How to Calculate:**

1. Rent/mortgage
2. Utilities
3. Transportation
4. Insurance
5. Basic food and necessities

Add a buffer. That's your MVI.

***Strategy:*** If you have a high-earning month, save the extra. If you fall below MVI, adjust immediately.

**Section VI: Smoothing the Spikes**

*Analogy (Dancers):* You can't always control the music. But you can control your form.

**Tips to Level Income Flow:**

- Offer retainers to clients (monthly payment plans)
- Diversify income: merch, digital downloads, courses
- Use contract deposits to secure income in advance

***Rule of Thumb:*** Make high months stretch. Never spend feast like famine won't follow.

**Section VII: Budgeting Tools for Irregular Income**

**Apps & Tools:**

- YNAB (You Need A Budget)
- Mint
- Google Sheets with custom formulas
- Cushion (for expense smoothing)

**Tips:**

- Budget by week, not month

- Forecast income from current bookings
- Always overestimate expenses

**Section VIII: Dealing with Financial Droughts**

*Analogy (Writers):* Not every season is a publishing season. Learn to write anyway.

**During Dry Spells:**

- Switch to bare-bones MVI mode
- Cut discretionary spending immediately
- Hustle for quick cash: sell gear, offer flash sales, take side gigs

***Action Step:*** Make a "famine protocol" for your business. Write down what cuts first.

**Section IX: Preventing Feast Mentality Overspending**

*Analogy (Filmmakers):* Don't blow your entire budget on the first scene.

**Tactics:**

- Auto-transfer 30% of any payment into savings
- Wait 7 days before big purchases
- Review your budget before every new gig

***Rule of Thumb:*** Treat every big check like a quarterly budget, not a payday.

**Section X: Long-Term Budgeting Strategy**

*Analogy (Sculptors):* Chip away at your goals bit by bit.

**Yearly Budget Tips:**

- Track seasonality: When are your busy months?
- Save during hot seasons for cold ones
- Set quarterly income targets

***Action Step:*** Make a 12-month cash flow calendar

**Conclusion: Stability Is the Real Flex**

Being an artist doesn't mean being broke. And budgeting doesn't mean restriction. It means direction.

When you budget with intention, you:

- Say yes to aligned work
- Say no to desperation gigs
- Make room for rest, creativity, and growth

You can build consistency inside chaos. You just need rhythm, routine, and the right tools.

Start today. Start small. Start with your next payment.

Let your budget be your creative partner—not your prison.

Because real freedom? That's being able to choose your gigs, protect your peace, and fund your future.

# Chapter 8: Personal vs. Business Finances

*Separate Accounts, Clear Records, and Peace of Mind for Artists*

For artists, creativity often spills into every part of life—your studio is in your apartment, your laptop is for both design gigs and family emails, your car hauls gear and groceries. But when your money gets tangled the same way, confusion leads to chaos.

One of the most powerful shifts you can make as an artist is learning to **separate your personal and business finances**. It doesn't just make taxes easier. It brings peace of mind, clarity, professionalism, and more control over your financial future.

**Section I: Why Artists Blend Personal and Business Finances**

*Analogy (Painters):* Imagine mixing every color on one brush. No separation, no contrast. The final piece is mud. Your finances work the same way. If every dollar goes through the same channel, you can't see what's working.

**Common Reasons Creatives Mix Finances:**

- Freelance feels like "just a side hustle"
- Fear of setting up a business account
- Uncertainty about taxes or legal structure
- Belief that "I'll separate it later"

***Rule of Thumb:*** If you make money from your art, you already run a business—act like it.

**Section II: Business vs. Personal Money Defined**

**Personal Finances:** Rent, groceries, cell phone, Netflix, health insurance, clothes

**Business Finances:** Software subscriptions, website hosting, equipment, business meals, supplies, contractor payments, travel to a shoot or performance

*Analogy (Photographers):* Think of your personal money as your camera bag and your business money as your camera body. You don't swap lenses blindly. Each has a purpose.

**Section III: Pros and Cons of Separation**

**Pros:**

- Clearer tax reporting
- Professionalism when working with clients
- Easier budgeting and savings goals
- Better financial decision-making
- Protects your personal assets if you form an LLC or corp

**Cons:**

- Requires extra setup (bank accounts, record-keeping)
- Can feel overwhelming at first
- Slight learning curve with financial tools

***Strategy:*** Start simple. One new account. One small change.

**Section IV: How to Set Up Separate Accounts**

***Step 1: Open a Business Checking Account***

- Choose a no-fee online bank or credit union
- Use your name if you're a sole proprietor
- Use your LLC name if you've formed one

***Step 2: Get a Business Savings Account***

- For taxes, emergency funds, and future investments

***Step 3: Redirect All Business Payments***

- PayPal, Venmo, Stripe, Zelle, checks—send them to your business account only

***Step 4: Pay Yourself a Salary or Transfer***

- Weekly, bi-weekly, or monthly
- This becomes your personal income

*Analogy (Writers):* Think of this system like chapters in a book. Each section has a function. Mixing them makes your plot confusing.

**Section V: Budgeting Separately**

**Business Budget Categories:**

- Office/studio rent
- Marketing
- Subscriptions and apps
- Art supplies and gear
- Continuing education
- Contract labor

**Personal Budget Categories:**

- Rent/mortgage
- Utilities
- Health insurance
- Food
- Personal savings goals

*Analogy (Dancers):* You choreograph movement in sequences. Same with money: business and personal have their own choreography.

***Action Step:*** Use two different budgeting tools or tabs. Don't combine.

**Section VI: Record-Keeping Basics**

***Rule of Thumb:*** Keep every receipt for business expenses. Use digital tools.

**Top Tools:**

- QuickBooks Self-Employed
- Wave Accounting (free)
- FreshBooks
- Google Drive for storing receipts
- Expensify

***Action Steps:***

1. Track income and expenses weekly
2. Store receipts in a monthly digital folder
3. Create an "End of Month" review ritual

**Section VII: Taxes and Legal Protections**

*Analogy (Actors):* You wouldn't perform without knowing your lines. Don't operate a creative business without understanding tax basics.

**Why Separation Matters for Taxes:**

- Makes deductions cleaner and less risky
- Easier to prove business losses or profits
- Can reduce audit risk

**Legal Reasons:**

- LLC or Corporation = limited liability
- Blending finances may "pierce the veil" and put your personal assets at

risk

***Action Step:*** Talk to a tax pro once per year to stay compliant and proactive

**Section VIII: Paying Yourself Like a Pro**

*Analogy (Musicians):* Touring, studio work, merch sales—different income streams. Your job is to convert inconsistent pay into reliable personal income.

**Pay Structure Ideas:**

- Pay yourself a flat amount each month
- Transfer a percentage of every payment
- Build a 3-month cash cushion to stabilize your pay

***Strategy:*** Build a system where business income stays in your business account until it pays *you*.

**Section IX: Scaling with Financial Clarity**

When your business and personal finances are cleanly separated:

- You can apply for business grants, loans, or credit cards
- You can hire contractors or assistants legally and clearly
- You can see what work is profitable vs. draining
- You can plan your year in quarters, not panic

*Analogy (Filmmakers):* A clean shoot starts with a clear shot list. Financial separation is your shot list for creative growth.

**Section X: Final Rules of Thumb**

1. Separate early. Fixing a mess is harder than starting clean.
2. If it supports your ability to earn money, it's probably a business expense.
3. Review both business and personal budgets monthly.
4. Save at least 25–30% of business income for taxes.
5. Never use your personal account to pay business bills—even in

emergencies.

**Conclusion: Separate to Grow**

Keeping your personal and business finances separate is not just about bookkeeping. It's about boundaries, clarity, professionalism, and growth.

It means you know what's coming in, what's going out, and where your time and energy are best spent.

Start small. Open one new account. Track one week of income. Build from there.

Because once you separate your accounts, you stop treating your art like a hobby and start treating it like the powerful, professional vehicle it is.

**When you separate your money, you multiply your focus. And focus fuels freedom.**

# Chapter 9: Creating an Emergency Fund for the Unexpected

*Why This Is a Creative's Safety Net—and Your First Step Toward Financial Freedom*

If you're a working artist, chances are you already know the unexpected can hit at any time. Gigs cancel. Gear breaks. Health scares happen. Projects fall through. Algorithms change. Recessions strike. In a world where your income isn't fixed and your work doesn't come with a 401(k), **you need your own safety net**.

Enter the emergency fund.

An emergency fund isn't just a good idea. It's the foundation of financial peace of mind. It's what lets you say no to panic projects, take time off to heal or recalibrate, and pivot when life demands it.

This chapter will walk you through why emergency funds matter for artists, how to build one (even with unpredictable income), and how to use creative analogies to stay motivated and intentional as you grow it.

**Section I: What is an Emergency Fund?**

An emergency fund is a **stash of money** you set aside specifically for unexpected expenses. It's not an investment. It's not for vacations. It's not for slow months or non-emergency business costs. It's your **financial fire extinguisher**.

***Rule of Thumb:*** Save 3–6 months of essential expenses in a separate, easy-to-access account.

*Analogy (Photographers):* It's like carrying extra batteries, backup SD cards, and a second lens. You might not need them—but when you do, you're grateful.

*Analogy (Musicians):* Your emergency fund is your backup amp. Your gear might fail mid-set. But the show goes on if you're prepared.

*Analogy (Dancers):* It's like warming up before rehearsal. You're preventing injury—protecting the asset that is YOU.

*Analogy (Writers):* Think of it as an unpublished piece. You don't need it yet, but it's your fallback when you hit writer's block or need to pause pitching.

**Section II: Why Artists Need Emergency Funds More Than Most**

1. **Unpredictable Income**: You can't guarantee next month's earnings.
2. **Seasonal Workflows**: Creative gigs often come in waves.
3. **No Traditional Safety Net**: No employer-funded sick leave, disability, or severance.
4. **Freelance Volatility**: Clients ghost. Events cancel. Markets shift.
5. **Mental Health & Burnout**: Taking a break shouldn't destroy your finances.

***Action Step:*** Make a list of 5 emergencies that would disrupt your life. Use this to stay motivated.

**Section III: How Much Should You Save?**

***Rule of Thumb:*** Start with **$500**. Then aim for **1 month**, **3 months**, and eventually **6 months** of expenses.

**Break It Down:**

- Rent/Mortgage
- Utilities
- Insurance (health, car, gear)
- Transportation
- Food
- Minimum debt payments
- Internet/Phone (essential for work)

*Action Step:* Calculate your "bare-bones monthly budget." Multiply by 3 to get your Phase 1 emergency goal.

**Section IV: Where to Keep It**

***Strategy:*** Keep it safe, separate, and accessible—but not *too* accessible.

**Best Options:**

- High-yield savings account
- Online bank with no debit card
- Credit union with easy transfer access

**Avoid:**

- Keeping it in checking (too tempting to spend)
- Investing it (you need liquidity, not risk)

*Analogy (Filmmakers):* It's your B-roll. You don't cut it into every scene, but it's there to save the story.

**Section V: How to Build One on an Irregular Income**

**1. Use Percentages Instead of Fixed Amounts**

Save **10% of every payment** that comes in, no matter how small.

**2. Automate the Transfer**

Even $5 a week adds up. Set up an auto-transfer from your checking to your emergency fund.

**3. Create a Line Item in Your Budget**

Treat savings like rent. It's not optional.

**4. Use Windfalls Wisely**

Got a grant, tax refund, or big commission? Put at least 25% into your emergency fund.

***Action Step:*** Go through your last 3 months of income. What could you have saved if you applied the 10% rule?

**Section VI: Pros and Cons of Emergency Funds**

**Pros:**

- Prevents debt during crisis
- Reduces anxiety
- Helps you say "no" to low-paying gigs
- Creates stability during slow seasons
- Allows you to rest when needed

**Cons:**

- Can feel slow to build
- Takes discipline not to dip into it
- Harder to prioritize when you're barely making ends meet

***Rule of Thumb:*** Progress > perfection. Small consistent steps build big peace of mind.

**Section VII: What Counts as an Emergency?**

**Valid Uses:**

- Medical expenses
- Urgent home/car repairs
- Replacing stolen or broken tools of your trade
- Job or income loss
- Temporary relocation or support

**NOT Valid:**

- Vacations
- Gear upgrades
- Holiday gifts
- Eating out
- Paying for a gig upfront

***Action Step:*** Write a list of YOUR approved emergency fund uses. Keep it near the account.

**Section VIII: When to Use It—and When Not To**

***Strategy:*** Only use your emergency fund when:

- The expense is urgent, necessary, and unexpected
- There is no other way to cover it
- You have a recovery plan in place

*Analogy (Designers):* You don't redesign the whole layout because of one comment. Emergency funds are for design emergencies, not tweaks.

*Analogy (Actors):* It's your understudy—don't bring them on unless you truly can't go on.

**Section IX: Rebuilding After a Withdrawal**

**Rule:** Use it, then **refill it immediately.**

**Steps:**

1. Pause nonessential spending
2. Cut discretionary categories
3. Pick up extra gigs if possible
4. Rebuild monthly until it's back

*Analogy (Musicians):* It's like replacing broken strings before your next gig. Don't wait. Re-string.

**Section X: Turning Emergency Funds Into Creative Freedom**

This isn't just about being "responsible." It's about:

- Taking a month off to write, paint, or rehearse
- Saying no to toxic clients
- Covering medical leave or family emergencies
- Traveling for inspiration without going broke
- Taking a class to upskill without financial panic

*Analogy (Sculptors):* You chisel away to create form. Emergency savings carves space in your life for control.

### Final Rules of Thumb

1. Save consistently, not perfectly.
2. Make it automatic.
3. Name the account something motivational.
4. Start with $500. Then $1,000. Then 3 months. Then 6.
5. Review your progress monthly.

### Conclusion: Build Your Cushion Before You Need It

Financial freedom for artists doesn't begin with grants, fame, or a full-time gig. It begins with a **cushion.**

An emergency fund won't solve everything—but it buys you something invaluable: **time, choice, peace, and creative power.**

Because when life happens (and it will), you shouldn't have to choose between survival and your calling.

Protect your art. Build your fund.

One dollar at a time.

One step closer to freedom.

# Chapter 10: Understanding Credit and Managing Debt

*Credit Cards, Scores, and Borrowing Wisely for Creative Professionals*

As a creative, your tools are often tangible: a brush, a camera, a mic, your voice, your body. Credit, on the other hand, feels abstract—until it doesn't.

One moment you're applying for a grant, renting a studio, or booking a hotel for a festival. The next, you're denied because of a number you didn't even know you had: your credit score.

Debt and credit aren't just banking buzzwords. They're **tools**—and like any tool, they can either build something powerful or cause serious damage. In this chapter, we'll demystify the world of credit and debt, and walk through exactly how artists can borrow smartly, protect their credit, and use both to create—not collapse.

**Section I: What Is Credit, Really?**

**Definition:** Credit is your ability to borrow money with the promise to pay it back later, often with interest.

**Why It Matters:** Credit history determines your access to loans, housing, cars, and even jobs. A good credit score = more opportunities, better rates, lower stress.

**Analogy (Photographers):** Credit is like your camera sensor. It silently shapes the quality of your results. If it's dirty, blurry, or ignored, every shot is affected.

**Analogy (Actors):** Think of your credit like your professional reputation.

Even if you're talented, if you're late, unreliable, or have a bad review, it affects what jobs you land.

**Section II: Understanding Credit Scores**

**Score Range:** 300 to 850

**Excellent:** 750+

**Good:** 700–749

**Fair:** 650–699

**Poor:** 600–649

**Very Poor:** Below 600

**What Makes Up Your Score?**

1. **Payment History (35%)** – On-time payments are the #1 factor
2. **Credit Utilization (30%)** – How much you use vs. how much you have
3. **Length of Credit History (15%)** – Older accounts = better
4. **Types of Credit (10%)** – Mix of loans and cards
5. **New Credit (10%)** – How many recent inquiries or accounts you've opened

***Rule of Thumb:*** Keep your credit utilization below 30%. Under 10% is ideal.

**Section III: Credit Cards—Friend or Foe?**

**Pros:**

- Builds credit history
- Earns rewards or cashback
- Offers fraud protection
- Can be used for emergencies

**Cons:**

- High interest rates
- Easy to overspend
- Missed payments damage credit

**Strategy:**

- Only use credit cards for **budgeted** expenses (bills, gas, groceries)
- Pay off in full each month
- Use auto-pay to avoid late fees

*Analogy (Musicians):* A credit card is like a tour van. It can help you cover ground faster—but if you don't maintain it, it'll break down and leave you stranded.

**Section IV: Debt—Types, Risks, and Responsibilities**

**Types of Debt:**

- **Good Debt:** Student loans (if used well), business loans, a mortgage
- **Bad Debt:** High-interest credit cards, payday loans, unneeded financing

*Analogy (Painters):* Debt is like painting with oils. If you layer too fast without control, it becomes a muddy mess. But used carefully? It creates lasting impact.

***Rule of Thumb:*** Never borrow money for something that won't generate value, income, or growth.

**Action Steps:**

1. List all your debts, interest rates, and monthly payments
2. Choose a payoff method: Snowball (smallest balance first) or Avalanche (highest interest first)
3. Pay more than the minimum when you can

**Section V: Managing Credit Like a Pro**

**Tips:**

- Don't close your oldest credit card
- Apply for new credit sparingly

- Review your credit report annually at AnnualCreditReport.com
- Set up due date reminders or automatic payments

**Strategy:**

- Keep one card just for subscriptions or business expenses
- Use another only for emergencies (but still pay in full)

*Analogy (Dancers):* Credit is choreography. Every movement (payment) needs to be in sync, or the entire routine falls apart.

**Section VI: When to Use Credit—And When Not To**

**Use Credit For:**

- Business expenses with a plan for repayment
- Building or repairing credit
- Emergencies (if no cash buffer exists)

**Avoid Using Credit For:**

- Vacations you can't afford
- Buying gear just to "keep up"
- Covering routine living expenses without a repayment plan

***Rule of Thumb:*** If you wouldn't be able to pay it back in 30–60 days, don't charge it.

**Section VII: Debt Payoff Plans for Artists**

**1. Debt Snowball (Psychological Win)**

- Pay smallest debt first
- Builds motivation

**2. Debt Avalanche (Interest Win)**

- Pay highest-interest first
- Saves the most money

**3. Hybrid Strategy**

- Mix small wins with high-interest focus

*Analogy (Writers):* Think of debt like editing. Some cuts (small debts) are quick and satisfying. Others (high-interest) make the most impact.

***Action Step:*** Create a tracker for your debts. Visualize your progress with a bar graph or checklist.

**Section VIII: Borrowing to Build—Not Bury**

**When It Makes Sense:**

- To invest in education or skills that lead to higher income
- To grow a business (if revenue projections support it)
- To buy time (a short-term loan while waiting on confirmed payments)

**When It Doesn't:**

- Emotional spending
- Trying to impress others
- Believing "you'll figure it out later"

*Analogy (Filmmakers):* You wouldn't film on credit with no script or distribution plan. Borrowing should be backed by strategy.

**Section IX: Building Credit from Scratch (or Repairing It)**

**If You Have No Credit:**

- Open a secured credit card
- Become an authorized user on someone else's card
- Use credit builder loans

**If You Have Bad Credit:**

- Don't avoid it—start rebuilding
- Set up payment plans
- Use apps like Self, Kikoff, or Experian Boost

***Action Step:*** Pull your credit report. Dispute errors. Track your score monthly using free tools like Credit Karma.

**Section X: Final Rules of Thumb**

1. Credit is a tool, not a crutch
2. Always know your balance and due date
3. Use less than 30% of your credit limit
4. Don't borrow without a repayment plan
5. You are not your credit score
6. A $10 paid-on-time bill builds credit better than a $1,000 late one
7. Protect your peace—don't co-sign unless you can pay it yourself

**Conclusion: Credit Can Build, Debt Can Empower—If You Master Them**

Artists deserve access to all the tools that support their growth. Credit is one of them. Managed wisely, it can help you:

- Fund creative opportunities
- Stabilize uneven cash flow
- Launch your next phase

But unmanaged? It becomes a weight that dims your creative energy.

You are already skilled at working with abstract tools—light, sound, story, movement. Credit is no different.

Learn the rhythm. Build the discipline. Rewrite your credit narrative.

Because freedom isn't just about time. It's about financial control—and credit done right gives you more of both.

# Chapter 11: Understanding Artist Income Streams

*Commissions, Royalties, Sales, Gigs, Licensing, and Freelancing—Decoded for Creative Professionals*

Every artist knows that relying on a single income stream is like painting with only one color. The real magic happens when you layer. In today's creative economy, financial sustainability comes not from one big break—but from **multiple reliable, recurring income sources** that together build your freedom.

This chapter explores the various ways artists make money and how to build a layered income portfolio that reflects your medium, your rhythm, and your values.

Whether you're a photographer booking weddings, a musician streaming on Spotify, a visual artist selling prints, or a dancer teaching choreography classes, we'll explore what income options you have, how to track them, grow them, and combine them strategically.

**Section I: Core Income Streams for Artists**

1. **Commissions** – Client-specific work, often custom and high-touch.

- *Photographers:* Family sessions, headshots
- *Painters:* Portraits, murals
- *Writers:* Ghostwriting, corporate copywriting

1. **Sales** – One-time transactions of your work or product.

- *Musicians:* Albums, vinyl, merch
- *Designers:* Logos, brand kits
- *Artists:* Paintings, ceramics, fashion

1. **Royalties** – Ongoing payments for past work used repeatedly.

- *Musicians:* Streaming platforms, radio
- *Authors:* Book sales, licensing
- *Visual Artists:* Print-on-demand platforms, stock art

1. **Gigs** – Live performances or time-specific appearances.

- *Actors:* Theatre, commercials
- *Musicians:* Shows, weddings, studio sessions
- *Dancers:* Live shows, music videos

1. **Freelancing** – Short-term or contract-based creative labor.

- *Designers:* Web design, branding projects
- *Photographers:* Event work, editorial shoots
- *Writers:* Articles, editing, marketing content

1. **Licensing** – Granting others the right to use your work.

- *Visual artists:* Apparel prints, gallery reproduction
- *Filmmakers:* Footage licensing
- *Musicians:* Sync licensing for film, TV, ads

1. **Teaching/Coaching** – Passing on your craft.

- *Musicians:* Private lessons

- *Dancers:* Masterclasses
- *Painters:* Workshops, virtual art classes

1. **Affiliate/Passive Income** – Earnings from promoting tools, platforms, or creating scalable products.

- *Photographers:* Lightroom presets
- *Designers:* Figma templates
- *Artists:* Online courses, YouTube content

## Section II: Rules of Thumb for Managing Creative Income Streams

1. Don't rely on one income stream—aim for at least **3 active** and **1 passive**.
2. Focus on building **recurring** revenue—like royalties or retainers.
3. Use **active income** to fund **passive income development**.
4. Track each stream separately to see what's profitable.
5. Treat your art like a business. Pay yourself from each stream.

## Section III: Action Steps to Identify & Grow Your Streams

1. List all current ways you earn money from your art.
2. Categorize each as active, semi-passive, or passive.
3. Analyze: Which pay the most? Which drain you?
4. Identify 1 new income stream to build in the next 90 days.
5. Set a goal: "I want X to earn $500/month by [date]."

## Section IV: Pros and Cons of Each Stream

**Commissions:**

- *Pros:* High pay, client relationships
- *Cons:* Custom, time-intensive, no reuse

**Sales:**

- *Pros:* Scalable, can batch-create
- *Cons:* Income varies, requires marketing

**Royalties:**

- *Pros:* Long-term passive income
- *Cons:* Often low unless volume is high

**Gigs:**

- *Pros:* Fast income, exposure
- *Cons:* Requires your time, often not repeatable

**Freelancing:**

- *Pros:* Contracted, predictable
- *Cons:* Deadline pressure, can crowd out personal projects

**Licensing:**

- *Pros:* Scales your work across platforms
- *Cons:* Legal contracts needed, slow to grow

**Teaching:**

- *Pros:* Consistent, fulfilling
- *Cons:* Energy-intensive, requires prep

**Affiliate/Passive:**

- *Pros:* Income while you sleep

- *Cons:* Takes time and tech to build

**Section V: Artist-Specific Analogies for Income Clarity**

*Photographers:* Think of each income stream as a different lens. You wouldn't shoot every project with a wide-angle. Income diversity gives you creative depth.

*Actors:* You don't rely on one role to define your career. Gigs, voiceovers, commercials, and stage work combine to form your portfolio.

*Musicians:* You might make money from shows, streams, merch, and lessons. Each one adds harmony to your financial song.

*Painters:* Sales of originals are great, but prints, licensing, and classes give you reach.

*Writers:* Articles, books, editing, workshops—each line adds to your paragraph of financial strength.

**Section VI: Mixing Streams Into a Sustainable Strategy**

**1. The Portfolio Approach:**

- Like a gallery show: multiple works, different mediums

**2. Time-Bound Streams:**

- Gig-based = immediate cash
- Royalties = long-term stability

**3. Effort-Based Planning:**

- Teaching: high energy, high control
- Passive sales: high setup, low maintenance

**4. Risk-Spreading Strategy:**

- If gigs dry up, commissions hold
- If sales drop, licensing bridges the gap

***Rule of Thumb:*** Don't scale what drains you. Grow what fuels you.

**Section VII: Tracking & Managing Each Stream**

**Tools to Use:**

- Spreadsheet with tabs by stream
- QuickBooks or Wave for invoicing
- Notion or Airtable for pipeline tracking

**Track:**

- Income earned
- Time spent
- Expenses per stream
- ROI: Return on investment

***Action Step:*** Spend one day a month reviewing income by stream. Ask: What's worth repeating?

**Section VIII: Scaling Your Top Streams**

**1. Turn your most reliable gig into a subscription or retainer. 2. Turn popular classes into a digital course. 3. License your art instead of selling it once. 4. Collaborate to multiply reach.**

***Strategy:*** Scale what is proven. Don't add 10 new things. Go deeper on what works.

**Section IX: Creating an Artist Income Ecosystem**

Your streams should work **together**, not compete.

- Teaching drives sales.
- Sales fund licensing.
- Licensing builds your brand.
- Gigs expand your audience.

***Rule of Thumb:*** Every project should lead to the next opportunity. Build income into the system, not just the moment.

**Section X: Final Thoughts—Financial Fluidity is Freedom**

You don't need to monetize everything you make. But you do need a plan.

Financial literacy for artists starts with awareness—and ends with **architecture**. You are building something. Not just art, but income. Not just projects, but portfolios. Not just gigs, but systems.

Think of your income like a mixed-media piece: each layer adds dimension. Each stream gives you choice. And each check you earn on your terms becomes part of your masterpiece.

Build your streams. Watch your freedom rise.

# Chapter 12: Tracking Income and Expenses Like a Pro

*Tools, Tactics, and Analogies for Artists of Every Discipline to Gain Control of Their Money*

Tracking your income and expenses isn't about obsessing over numbers—it's about reclaiming your creative freedom. For artists, money often feels like an afterthought, a mystery, or a mess. But the truth is, every dollar you earn and every dollar you spend tells a story. And you, the artist, are the author.

This chapter is about learning to **track your finances with the same clarity and care you give your creative process**. When you track well, you budget better, make smarter decisions, and build a future you can depend on—without giving up your art.

Whether you're a freelance dancer, a self-published poet, a muralist, or a touring musician, this guide will help you understand where your money goes, how to track it, and why doing so transforms your entire financial (and creative) life.

**Section I: Why Tracking Matters for Artists**

1. **Income is Irregular.** Your paychecks vary. Tracking helps stabilize chaos.
2. **Expenses Are Overlooked.** Subscriptions, supply runs, promo costs—they add up fast.
3. **Taxes Get Complicated.** Good records = fewer headaches = more

write-offs.

4. **Business Growth Demands Data.** You can't scale what you don't measure.

**Analogy (Musicians):** Think of tracking like recording stems in a DAW (digital audio workstation). You isolate each track so you can adjust, improve, and harmonize. Money works the same way.

## Section II: Rules of Thumb for Tracking Like a Pro

1. Track **every** source of income—even bartered gigs or cash tips.
2. Separate personal and business spending.
3. Track in **real time**, not months later.
4. Automate what you can.
5. Schedule a **weekly money check-in**.
6. Keep receipts or digital logs of every expense.

## Section III: Action Steps to Build a Tracking System That Works

### Step 1: Choose Your Tool

- Spreadsheet (Google Sheets, Excel)
- Apps (Wave, QuickBooks Self-Employed, YNAB, Mint)
- Pen and paper journal
- Notion or Airtable template

### Step 2: Categorize Income Streams

- Commissions
- Royalties
- Gig pay
- Freelance contracts
- Digital product sales

### Step 3: Categorize Expenses

- Equipment & software
- Travel & gas
- Website & email tools
- Studio rent
- Printing & materials
- Marketing & promotion

**Step 4: Reconcile Weekly**

- Review accounts and categorize new income/expenses
- Label everything (project name, type, category)
- Check cash flow (net income = income - expenses)

**Step 5: Monthly Review**

- Look for trends
- What's growing?
- Where are you overspending?
- What stream is worth expanding?

**Section IV: Pros and Cons of Tracking Your Finances**

**Pros:**

- Peace of mind
- Better financial decisions
- Easier budgeting and saving
- Cleaner taxes and deductions
- Insight into what gigs/streams are truly profitable

**Cons:**

- Time-consuming at first
- Emotional discomfort (facing reality)

- Requires discipline and consistency

**Strategy:** Pair tracking with a weekly creative habit. Light a candle, grab a tea, and review your finances with the same mindset you'd prep a canvas or warm up for rehearsal.

**Section V: Artist-Specific Tracking Tips**

**Photographers:**

- Track gear depreciation, editing software, second shooters
- Use job numbers and client folders to tag expenses

**Musicians:**

- Log setlist payments, merch income, equipment repairs
- Track studio time vs. live gig costs

**Actors:**

- Record headshot costs, classes, coaching, auditions
- Track travel mileage for castings

**Visual Artists:**

- Tag by collection or exhibit
- Note cost of canvas, paints, framing, shipping

**Writers:**

- Categorize earnings by publisher or platform
- Note subscriptions: Grammarly, Substack, Scrivener

**Dancers:**

- Track rehearsal space rental, costumes, lessons
- Document performance stipends and teaching pay

**Filmmakers:**

- Budget shoots by line item
- Track licensing fees, editing software, crew payments

## Section VI: Using Your Data to Make Smarter Decisions

### 1. Evaluate Gigs and Clients

- How much did you actually earn *after* costs?
- Was the project worth the time?

### 2. Set Minimum Pay Rates

- Use past data to decide your bottom line

### 3. Create Forecasts

- Predict future earnings based on past months

### 4. Plan for Taxes

- Estimate quarterly tax payments based on real numbers

### 5. Build Reserves

- Set aside a percentage of each payment into savings

## Section VII: Top Tools for Artists

**General Tracking:**

- Google Sheets / Excel
- Notion templates

**Income & Expense Apps:**

- Wave (free, artist-friendly)
- QuickBooks Self-Employed
- FreshBooks
- Bonsai (for contracts + invoicing)

**Mileage/Receipts:**

- MileIQ
- Expensify
- Shoeboxed

**Integrated Tools for Artists:**

- Artful, Artwork Archive (for visual artists)
- Soundcharts, Songtrust (for musicians)
- Reedsy, Substack (for writers)

## Section VIII: Your Creative Finance Ritual

### Weekly Ritual:

- 15 min tracking
- Categorize & label expenses
- Note what worked (or didn't) financially this week

### Monthly Ritual:

- Run a "P&L" (Profit and Loss)
- Set a mini goal: increase merch sales, cut software costs, etc.

**Quarterly Ritual:**

- Review all income streams
- Rank top earners
- Adjust time/effort accordingly

**Annual Ritual:**

- File taxes with confidence
- Reflect on your financial growth
- Set goals for next year

### Section IX: How Tracking Builds Artist Wealth

- Empowers you to price better
- Reveals hidden income killers
- Shows which gigs to scale or drop
- Makes you eligible for loans or grants
- Prepares you for business growth

***Analogy (Painters):*** Each transaction is a brushstroke. Only by stepping back and reviewing the canvas can you understand the full picture.

### Conclusion: Track What Matters, and Watch It Grow

Artists track progress all the time—drafts, sketches, rehearsals, raw takes. Money is no different. Tracking isn't the opposite of creativity—it's the fuel that sustains it.

Start small. Pick a tool. Build your system. Commit to a rhythm. Soon, you'll feel more powerful, more informed, and more in control of your art—and your income.

**Because when you track your money like a pro, you protect your purpose like an artist.**

# Chapter 13: How to Get Paid and Invoice Professionally

*Net 30, Payment Platforms, and Client Boundaries for Creative Professionals*

As a creative, the joy is in the making—but let's be honest, the stress is often in the money. From unclear rates to late payments to vague project terms, artists across disciplines struggle with getting paid fairly, fully, and on time. This chapter is your blueprint to fix that.

Professional invoicing isn't about becoming a number-cruncher—it's about protecting your craft. When you set clear payment terms, use proper tools, and communicate with confidence, you eliminate ambiguity, reduce conflict, and step fully into your role as both artist and business owner.

**Section I: Why Payment Systems Matter for Artists**

1. **You Deserve Consistent Income** Art is unpredictable enough. Your systems shouldn't be.
2. **Getting Paid Late = Unnecessary Stress** Time spent chasing clients = time lost creating.
3. **Invoicing = Proof of Value** A clean, branded invoice says, "I take this seriously—and you should too."

**Analogy (Photographers):** A blurry contract is like a blurry photo. If you don't capture it clearly upfront, everything after is out of focus.

**Analogy (Musicians):** Think of invoicing like setting the tempo. You set the rhythm of the relationship—and you decide the beat.

**Section II: Rules of Thumb for Getting Paid Like a Pro**

1. Always have a written agreement or contract.
2. Send a professional invoice within 24–48 hours of project completion.
3. Include due dates, late fees, and payment terms on every invoice.
4. Request deposits for projects over $300–$500.
5. Avoid "net 60" or open-ended payment terms unless you're dealing with corporate clients.
6. Set payment boundaries before work begins.
7. Chase invoices with grace—but follow up consistently.

**Section III: Action Steps to Set Up Your Payment System**

**1. Choose Your Invoicing Platform:**

- **Wave (Free, artist-friendly)**
- **QuickBooks Self-Employed**
- **FreshBooks**
- **HoneyBook (for creatives)**
- **Bonsai (freelancer contracts + payments)**

**2. Create a Branded Invoice Template:**

- Include your name/logo, address, and contact info
- Assign invoice numbers for tracking
- List services with descriptions and rates
- Add totals, taxes (if applicable), and payment options

**3. Decide on Payment Terms:**

- "Net 7," "Net 14," or "Net 30" = # of days after invoice that payment is due
- Add late fees (e.g., 2% per 30 days overdue)

- Offer discounts for early payment if helpful (e.g., "2% off if paid within 5 days")

**4. Accept Multiple Payment Methods:**

- PayPal, Venmo Business, Zelle, Square, Stripe, direct deposit
- Avoid personal Venmo/PayPal to protect tax documentation and professionalism

**5. Draft a Short Payment Policy:**

- Send to all new clients
- Include terms, turnaround time, deposit requirements, and payment methods

**Section IV: Pros and Cons of Different Payment Terms**

**Net 7–14 (1–2 weeks):**

- *Pros:* Encourages faster cash flow
- *Cons:* Some clients may default if not used to it

**Net 30:**

- *Pros:* Standard in many industries
- *Cons:* Still requires chasing and reminders

**Due Upon Receipt:**

- *Pros:* Immediate action
- *Cons:* Not always realistic for larger projects

**Strategy:** Use **Net 7** for new or individual clients, **Net 30** for agencies or institutions. Set up automated reminders 3–5 days before due dates.

## Section V: Artist-Specific Payment Practices

### Photographers:

- Request 50% upfront, 50% upon delivery
- Watermark images until balance is paid

### Painters/Sculptors:

- Split payments: Design fee, material cost, delivery
- Use milestone invoices for large works

### Musicians/DJs:

- Require deposit to hold date
- Balance due before performance begins

### Actors/Performers:

- Use standard SAG/AFTRA contracts when possible
- Always invoice for rehearsals + prep time

### Writers/Editors:

- Use contracts outlining rounds of revision
- Include research hours as line items

### Designers/Filmmakers:

- Use contracts with kill fees, revision limits
- Require staged payments: concept, draft, final

## Section VI: Using Invoicing Tools Efficiently

### Automation Tips:

- Auto-send invoices after project milestones
- Set auto-reminders for due dates
- Sync with accounting software or bank

**Tracking Tips:**

- Use invoice numbers sequentially
- Keep a separate "Past Due" tracking file
- Tag by client, project type, or timeline

**Follow-Up Script Template:** "Hi [Client],

Just a quick follow-up on invoice #[XXX] sent on [DATE]. The due date was [DUE DATE]. Please let me know if you need a re-send or have any questions.

Appreciate your time and look forward to resolving this soon!

Best, [Your Name]"

**Section VII: Setting Client Boundaries and Protecting Yourself**

**1. No work starts without a deposit. 2. Limit revision rounds and outline them in writing. 3. Add kill fees to cover canceled projects. 4. Be clear about rush fees (e.g., +25% for <48 hr turnaround). 5. Send contracts even for friends/family discounts.**

*Analogy (Dancers):* Boundaries in payment are like stage markers in choreography—they keep you from falling off the edge.

*Analogy (Writers):* You wouldn't submit a piece without a word count or deadline. Your pay should have parameters too.

**Section VIII: Avoiding Common Mistakes**

- Don't send vague invoices (e.g., "Creative work – $500")
- Don't delay sending the invoice—it delays your pay
- Don't work without a signed contract or email confirmation
- Don't be afraid to follow up—you're running a business

**Section IX: Handling Late or Non-Payers**

1. **Stay Professional.** Always lead with politeness. Follow with clarity.
2. **Use Written Follow-Ups.** Paper trail = protection
3. **Offer Payment Plans if Necessary.** Especially for small clients or one-offs
4. **Enforce Late Fees.** If you say you will—follow through
5. **Use a Collections Clause.** State: "If unpaid after 60 days, a 10% collection fee applies."
6. **Consider Small Claims Court (if over $500)** Or let it go and never work with them again

### Section X: Final Rules of Thumb

1. Always invoice clearly, quickly, and completely.
2. List services, rates, hours, and deliverables.
3. Set payment terms early and reinforce often.
4. Offer multiple payment options.
5. Create systems to reduce the emotion in follow-ups.
6. Save every invoice, receipt, and email.
7. Communicate like a pro—even when you're mad.

### Conclusion: Money Talks—So Learn to Speak Artist-CEO

You're not "just" an artist. You're a creative entrepreneur. And like any professional, you deserve clarity, consistency, and compensation.

Getting paid is more than a transaction—it's a boundary. It's a signal to the world that your time, talent, and energy matter.

Build your payment process like you build your art: with care, intention, and a clear vision.

Because when you invoice like a pro, you stop chasing checks and start designing your own financial rhythm—and nothing sounds sweeter than being paid well for what you love to do.

# Chapter 14: Financial Tools for Every Type of Artist

*Apps, Spreadsheets, and Accounting Systems to Help You Thrive Creatively and Financially*

As an artist, you already use tools every day. Brushes. Cameras. Words. Instruments. Choreography. Light. Sound. Texture.

But what about your financial tools?

The truth is, **the right financial tools can do for your money what your favorite brush does for your canvas**—make things clear, consistent, and creative. Whether you're a freelance filmmaker or a full-time muralist, a spoken word poet or a session drummer, having tools to track, manage, and grow your income is essential.

This chapter breaks down the best financial tools for different types of artists, how to use them, what to avoid, and how to build a workflow that supports your art—not stifles it.

**Section I: Why Artists Need Financial Tools**

1. **Inconsistent Income** demands systems that smooth out cash flow.
2. **Tax Season** shouldn't feel like detective work.
3. **Project Budgets** are essential for scaling and pricing.
4. **Time = Money**—automation gives you back both.

**Analogy (Photographers):** Just like Lightroom presets speed up your editing, financial tools streamline your money habits.

**Analogy (Musicians):** Like a looping pedal—you can build on top of what you've already recorded.

**Analogy (Dancers):** Think of tools as your routine warm-up. It's what makes your movement more fluid and sustainable.

**Section II: Rules of Thumb for Using Financial Tools Wisely**

1. Start simple—tools should reduce stress, not add to it.
2. Choose tools that match your style: visual, detailed, minimalist.
3. Always test a tool for 30 days before committing.
4. Prioritize automation for repetitive tasks (invoicing, reminders).
5. Combine no more than 3 tools for most workflows.

**Section III: Essential Financial Tool Categories**

1. **Income & Expense Tracking**
2. **Invoicing & Payments**
3. **Budgeting & Forecasting**
4. **Project Management & Time Tracking**
5. **Mileage, Receipts & Deductions**
6. **Tax & Accounting Software**
7. **Digital Banking & Payment Platforms**

**Section IV: Top Tools for Income & Expense Tracking**

**Spreadsheets**

- Google Sheets / Excel templates (customizable, free)
- Best for visual artists, writers, and those who want full control

**Apps**

- **Wave** (free, easy invoicing + expense tracking)
- **QuickBooks Self-Employed** (automated mileage + quarterly tax estimates)

- **FreshBooks** (great for creatives with multiple clients)

**Pros:**

- Customizable, gives clarity
- Helps prepare for taxes
- Essential for tracking profitability

**Cons:**

- Requires maintenance
- Some learning curve

**Section V: Invoicing & Payments Platforms**
**Key Tools:**

- **HoneyBook** (designed for creative freelancers)
- **Bonsai** (contracts + proposals + payments)
- **Stripe** (for ecommerce or digital product sales)
- **Square** (POS + online invoicing)

**Artist Analogy (Painters):** Invoicing tools are your frame—they make the piece presentable, portable, and ready for sale.

***Rule of Thumb:*** Always have a reusable, branded invoice template linked to your chosen platform.

**Section VI: Budgeting & Forecasting Tools**

**Apps:**

- **YNAB (You Need A Budget):** great for irregular income
- **EveryDollar:** visual and simple
- **Tiller:** syncs banking with Google Sheets

**Use Case:**

- Set monthly spending caps
- Forecast big expenses (travel, gear, studio rent)

**Artist Analogy (Filmmakers):** Think of your budget like a shot list—it tells your project where to go and what to avoid wasting.

**Section VII: Project Management & Time Tracking**

**Tools:**

- **Toggl:** for tracking hours per client/project
- **Asana/Trello/Notion:** great for managing commissions, deadlines, and project phases

**Strategy:** Use these to calculate per-project ROI. If a commission takes 20 hours and pays $300, it may not be worth repeating.

**Artist Analogy (Actors):** Think of these as your rehearsal calendar—they tell you where to be and when.

**Section VIII: Mileage, Receipts & Deductions**

**Apps:**

- **MileIQ** (auto-tracks drives)
- **Expensify** (receipt management)
- **Shoeboxed** (scan receipts, track by category)

***Rule of Thumb:*** Save digital copies of all receipts. Categorize by event, client, or art show.

**Section IX: Tax & Accounting Tools**

**Software:**

- **TurboTax Self-Employed**
- **H&R Block Self-Employed**
- **Keeper Tax** (text-based expense tracking for freelancers)

**Why It Matters:**

- Helps estimate quarterly taxes
- Identifies deductible expenses
- Links with income tools

**Artist Analogy (Writers):** Tax tools are like editors. They catch what you miss—and save you from bad reviews (aka audits).

**Section X: Digital Banking & Payment Options**

**Platforms:**

- **Bluevine / Novo** (digital business banking)
- **PayPal Business / Venmo Business / Zelle**
- **Relay** (great for multiple accounts: taxes, savings, bills)

***Rule of Thumb:*** Keep at least 3 accounts: income, expenses, taxes.

**Artist Analogy (Dancers):** Each account is a partner. You need them to stay in sync to avoid stepping on toes.

**Section XI: Workflow Examples by Artist Type**

**Photographer:**

- Wave (invoicing + tracking)
- MileIQ (travel deductions)
- Google Sheets (shoot planner)

**Musician:**

- FreshBooks (studio sessions, gig payments)
- QuickBooks SE (track royalties, merch sales)
- Notion (tour and setlist planner)

**Painter:**

- Square (POS + invoice art sales)
- Excel (supply costs, exhibit fees)

- Tiller (monthly forecast)

**Dancer/Performer:**

- HoneyBook (class bookings + invoices)
- Expensify (costume, studio rental)
- Toggl (track rehearsals + admin)

**Writer/Editor:**

- Bonsai (contracts + editorial timelines)
- YNAB (budgeting between gigs)
- Reedsy (marketplace + client acquisition)

**Section XII: Building Your Custom Financial Dashboard**

**What to Track:**

- Monthly income by stream
- Monthly expenses by category
- Upcoming invoices due
- Tax savings progress
- Goals: new gear, travel, debt payoff

**How to Build It:**

- Use Notion, Airtable, or Google Sheets
- Create color-coded categories
- Set reminders

**Artist Analogy (Sculptors):** Your dashboard is your studio bench—everything organized, in view, ready to build.

**Conclusion: Tools Are Extensions of Your Vision**

You don't need to become an accountant to master your finances—you need the right tools to tell your story, control your time, and scale your art.

Choose tools that speak your language, mirror your style, and lighten your load. Your finances, like your art, deserve structure, support, and creative clarity.

**Because financial tools don't limit artists—they liberate them.**

Start with one tool. Learn it well. Then layer in more. Build a system that works for you—not against you.

Your money is part of your masterpiece. Give it the tools it needs to thrive.

# Chapter 15: Taxes 101 for Creatives

*Self-Employment Taxes, Deductions, and Write-Offs—Made for Artists by an Artist Who Gets It*

If the word "taxes" makes you want to hide behind your easel, slam your laptop shut, or run from the rehearsal studio—you're not alone.

For many creatives, taxes feel confusing, overwhelming, or just plain unfair. You're juggling unpredictable income, multiple gigs, and a pile of receipts that may or may not be in your glove compartment.

But here's the truth: **you don't have to become a CPA to take control of your taxes**. You just need to understand the basics—what you owe, what you can deduct, and how to prepare.

This chapter is your creative-friendly guide to managing taxes with clarity and confidence. Whether you're a painter, actor, musician, filmmaker, photographer, dancer, or writer—this is your playbook.

**Section I: Understanding Self-Employment Taxes**

**If you earn income from your art, and you're not on someone else's payroll—you're self-employed.**

That means you're responsible for:

1. **Income tax** (federal + state)
2. **Self-employment tax** (which covers Social Security + Medicare)

***Rule of Thumb:*** Set aside **25–30%** of every freelance or creative payment for taxes.

**Analogy (Photographers):** Think of your taxes like a photo backup.

You wouldn't trust one SD card—taxes are you backing up your financial integrity.

**Self-Employment Tax Rate:** 15.3%

- 12.4% for Social Security
- 2.9% for Medicare

**Section II: What Counts as Taxable Income?**

- Gigs
- Commissions
- Product sales
- Digital downloads
- Royalties
- Tips
- Licensing fees

**Yes, even cash from your open mic night is taxable.**

***Action Step:*** Start tracking all income, even if it's inconsistent or under-the-table.

**Section III: What You Can (Legally) Write Off**

**Common Deductions for Artists:**

- Supplies (paint, brushes, film, costumes, etc.)
- Home office/studio space
- Phone, internet (portion used for business)
- Equipment (cameras, mics, laptops)
- Software (Adobe, DAWs, Final Cut, etc.)
- Website + domain + hosting
- Subscriptions (music, photography, creative tools)
- Marketing/promo costs (social ads, printing flyers)
- Education (workshops, classes)
- Travel (flights, hotels, gas for business trips)

- Meals (during business travel or client meetings)

**Analogy (Actors):** Think of write-offs like stage props. They support your performance—and if they're necessary for the role (your business), they're deductible.

**Section IV: Rules of Thumb for Creative Deductions**

1. It must be **ordinary and necessary** to your field.
2. It must be related to your art **as a business**.
3. You must keep **documentation** (receipts, logs, notes).

**Gray Areas:**

- Clothing is usually **not** deductible—unless it's a costume.
- Home utilities can be partially deductible—only the business portion.

***Strategy:*** Create three folders: digital receipts, physical receipts, and a tax log spreadsheet.

**Section V: Estimated Quarterly Taxes**

If you expect to owe more than $1,000 in taxes for the year, the IRS expects you to pay **quarterly**.

**Due Dates:**

- April 15
- June 15
- September 15
- January 15 (of the next year)

***Action Step:*** Set calendar reminders and set aside tax money monthly to avoid scrambling.

**Apps to Help:**

- QuickBooks Self-Employed

- Keeper Tax
- TaxAct
- IRS Direct Pay (to make payments online)

**Section VI: Artist Tax Prep Workflow (Quarterly + Yearly)**

**Monthly:**

- Track all income + expenses
- Log mileage, receipts, tips
- Auto-transfer tax money to separate account

**Quarterly:**

- Calculate earnings
- Submit estimated tax payments

**Annually:**

- Gather 1099s or total income summaries
- Finalize expense categories
- File your taxes (yourself or via a pro)

**Analogy (Musicians):** Think of tax prep like a rehearsal. If you practice consistently, the performance (filing season) is a lot smoother.

**Section VII: Working With a Tax Professional**

**Pros:**

- Saves time
- Catches deductions you may miss
- Ensures compliance
- Gives peace of mind

**Cons:**

- Costs more than DIY tools
- You still need to organize your records

***Strategy:*** Use a tax pro if:

- You earn more than $30,000/year from your art
- You have employees or subcontractors
- You're behind on filings

**Artist Analogy (Filmmakers):** Think of a CPA like your editor—they make sense of all the raw footage (receipts).

**Section VIII: Common Tax Mistakes Creatives Make**

1. Not filing because "I didn't earn much"
2. Not saving receipts
3. Forgetting to claim mileage
4. Paying late (and accruing penalties)
5. Mixing personal and business accounts
6. Not reporting cash income

***Rule of Thumb:*** If you're getting paid, assume it's taxable. And if it helps you earn, it might be deductible.

**Section IX: Setting Up Systems for Long-Term Tax Success**

**1. Open a separate checking account for your creative business. 2. Use one credit card for all art-related purchases. 3. Use an app or spreadsheet to track income/expenses weekly. 4. Keep digital and physical copies of receipts. 5. Review finances monthly so you're not scrambling at tax time.**

**Artist Analogy (Writers):** Tax systems are like outlining your book—it makes the draft (your filing) way easier.

**Section X: Pros and Cons of Being a Self-Employed Creative (Tax-Wise)**

**Pros:**

- You control your income sources
- More tax deductions than W-2 employees
- Flexible lifestyle

**Cons:**

- Must pay your own taxes + Medicare + Social Security
- No employer-provided benefits
- Higher audit risk if records are messy

***Strategy:*** Maximize deductions + automate savings + plan ahead.

**Conclusion: Taxes Aren't the Villain—Disorganization Is**

You're already managing dozens of moving parts in your creative career. Tracking gigs, emails, equipment, ideas—money is just one more system. The difference? It can empower you or overwhelm you.

Start small:

- Save receipts
- Track income weekly
- Open a business bank account
- Automate tax savings

Then grow your financial muscle. And if you're ever unsure? Ask for help. CPAs, apps, and communities exist to support you.

**Because your art deserves to thrive—and that starts with knowing your numbers.**

# Chapter 16: Quarterly Taxes — What They Are and How to Pay Them

*Avoiding IRS Surprises with the Confidence of a Creative CEO*

If tax time always sneaks up on you like a bad lighting cue or missed stage entrance, you're not alone. Many creatives don't realize they're supposed to be paying taxes four times a year—not just in April.

For freelancers, gig workers, and self-employed artists, quarterly estimated taxes are not just helpful—they're required. This chapter will break down exactly what quarterly taxes are, who needs to pay them, when to pay them, how to calculate them, and how to stay on top of it all without sacrificing your creative energy.

Whether you're a musician with multiple gigs, a filmmaker juggling projects, a painter selling originals, or a dancer teaching private lessons, this chapter is designed with you in mind.

**Section I: What Are Quarterly Taxes?**

Quarterly taxes are **estimated tax payments** made to the IRS four times a year. They include:

1. **Federal Income Tax**
2. **Self-Employment Tax** (Social Security and Medicare)

If you earn income **not subject to withholding**—like freelance gigs, royalties, or product sales—you likely owe quarterly taxes.

**Rule of Thumb:** If you expect to owe **more than $1,000** in federal taxes for the year, you're required to pay estimated taxes.

**Analogy (Musicians):** Think of quarterly taxes like sound checks before a gig. It prevents big problems later.

**Section II: Who Needs to Pay Quarterly Taxes?**

- Freelancers (writers, photographers, designers)
- Independent contractors (actors, musicians, editors)
- Gig workers (Uber, Fiverr, Etsy)
- Sole proprietors
- Small business owners
- Creators with Patreon, Substack, YouTube income

**If you're earning without a W-2, quarterly taxes are likely your responsibility.**

**Section III: When Are Quarterly Taxes Due?**

Quarterly tax payment schedule:

- **April 15** (for January–March income)
- **June 15** (for April–May income)
- **September 15** (for June–August income)
- **January 15** (of the next year—for September–December income)

***Strategy:*** Add reminders to your digital calendar with a two-week prep buffer.

**Analogy (Photographers):** Think of it like backing up your files regularly—you don't want to wait until you've lost everything.

**Section IV: How to Calculate Quarterly Taxes**

**Basic Formula:**

1. Estimate your total income for the year
2. Subtract your business expenses
3. Calculate 25–30% of your **net profit**

4. Divide by 4

**Tools to Use:**

- QuickBooks Self-Employed
- IRS Form 1040-ES
- Keeper Tax
- Tax calculator apps

**Rule of Thumb:** Overestimate slightly—better to get a refund than owe.

**Analogy (Painters):** Think of it like buying more canvas than you need. You'd rather have extra than run out mid-painting.

**Section V: How to Pay Quarterly Taxes**

**Methods:**

- **IRS Direct Pay** (https://www.irs.gov/payments)
- **EFTPS** (Electronic Federal Tax Payment System)
- **By check with IRS Form 1040-ES**
- **Tax software** (e.g., TurboTax, H&R Block, QuickBooks)

**State Taxes:**

- Check your state's Department of Revenue for estimated tax deadlines

**Strategy:** Open a separate savings account labeled "Taxes" and transfer 25–30% of each payment into it.

**Analogy (Writers):** Paying taxes as you go is like outlining your novel. It's harder to fix things at the end than to stay on track from the start.

**Section VI: Pros and Cons of Paying Quarterly Taxes**

**Pros:**

- Avoid large lump-sum tax bill
- Prevent interest + penalties

- Helps with budgeting and savings
- Keeps you in good standing with the IRS

**Cons:**

- Requires regular tracking
- Takes discipline
- Harder to manage if income is highly irregular

**Strategy Moving Forward:**

- Automate monthly savings for taxes
- Use a budget tool to plan ahead for slow months

**Section VII: What Happens If You Don't Pay?**

**Penalties Include:**

- Late payment penalties
- Interest on unpaid tax
- Increased audit risk

**Rule of Thumb:** It's better to pay *something* than nothing. Even partial payments reduce penalties.

**Analogy (Dancers):** Skipping quarterly taxes is like skipping warm-ups. Sooner or later, it catches up with you.

**Section VIII: Quarterly Tax Checklist for Creatives**

**Each Quarter:**

1. Review income earned
2. Subtract deductible expenses
3. Calculate 25–30% of the net
4. Submit payment via IRS or app
5. Log payment confirmation

**Monthly:**

- Track income and expenses in your spreadsheet or tool
- Label tax-deductible purchases

**Annually:**

- Compare estimates to actual income
- Adjust quarterly payments for accuracy

**Section IX: Tools and Apps to Make It Easier**

- **QuickBooks Self-Employed**: mileage, invoices, tax estimates
- **Keeper Tax**: AI finds deductions + sends reminders
- **Trello or Notion**: to create your own tax calendar
- **Wave**: free invoicing + payment tracking
- **IRS Direct Pay**: fast and secure way to pay directly

**Artist Analogy (Filmmakers):** These tools are like your editing software. They turn raw footage (invoices, receipts) into a clear, polished final product.

**Section X: Building Your Long-Term Tax Strategy**

1. **Treat Taxes Like a Bill.** Set it and forget it—transfer money each time you get paid.
2. **Pay Yourself a Salary.** Helps you plan spending and taxes.
3. **Create a Tax Folder (Digital & Physical).** Keep forms, receipts, payment confirmations.
4. **Schedule a Quarterly CEO Day.** Block 1 day each quarter to handle tax prep, review expenses, and pay estimates.

**Artist Analogy (Sculptors):** Tax planning is like carving. Every chisel now saves you from having to jackhammer later.

**Conclusion: Your Art Is Your Business—So Treat Taxes Like Part of**

**the Process**

Quarterly taxes may sound like a hassle, but they're actually your ally. They prevent surprises, build confidence, and give you the power to navigate your career with clarity.

Just like rehearsals, brushstrokes, edits, or takes—consistency creates the masterpiece. Stay in rhythm. Stay prepared.

And most of all—don't let taxes steal the spotlight from your art.

**Because financial readiness is part of your creative power.**

# Part III: Treating Your Art Like a Business

B*ringing Professional Structure to Your Creative Passion—Without Losing the Soul*

Artists often recoil at the word "business" like it's a creative buzzkill. But what if business wasn't the opposite of art—it was its frame, its amplifier, its launchpad?

Treating your art like a business doesn't mean selling out or chasing trends. It means creating systems, setting boundaries, charging your worth, and growing your reach **without compromising your integrity**.

In this section, we'll break down how to operate like a creative entrepreneur—tracking your time, pricing your work, managing clients, marketing your art, and making strategic decisions that support your sustainability.

Whether you're a choreographer, composer, sculptor, or illustrator, this guide will show you how to blend creative freedom with business intelligence.

**Section I: The Mindset Shift – Artist to Artist-CEO**

**Old Thinking:** "I'll make the work and hope someone buys it."

**New Thinking:** "I create art *and* build systems to sell, protect, and scale it."

**Analogy (Painters):** You wouldn't frame a masterpiece with duct tape. Why wrap your creative business in disorganization?

***Rule of Thumb:*** You are both the talent and the manager. Nurture both roles equally.

**Action Step:** Create a dual identity: [Your Name] the Artist and [Your

Name] the Business. Define what each one needs to thrive.

**Section II: Registering as a Legitimate Business**

**Sole Proprietor vs. LLC:**

- *Sole Proprietor:* Easy to set up, but no legal separation between you and your business.
- *LLC (Limited Liability Company):* Provides protection for personal assets and may add credibility.

**Action Steps:**

1. Check your state's website to register your business.
2. Apply for an EIN (Employer Identification Number) at IRS.gov.
3. Open a business checking account.

***Pros:***

- Legal protection
- Easier to apply for grants or loans
- Shows clients and galleries you're serious

**Analogy (Photographers):** Think of an LLC like a lens cap—it protects your most valuable gear.

**Section III: Pricing Your Work Like a Pro**

**Pricing Models:**

- Hourly rate (use for services like teaching, consulting)
- Per project (commissions, designs)
- Tiered pricing (original vs. print vs. merch)

***Rule of Thumb:*** Track how long things take. Include planning, admin, materials, and revisions.

**Action Step:** Create a rate card with base pricing and optional add-ons.

**Analogy (Musicians):** You charge not just for the concert—but the rehearsal, the gear, and the years of practice.

**Section IV: Tracking Your Time Like a Freelancer**

**Tools to Use:**

- Toggl
- Harvest
- Clockify

**Categories to Track:**

- Creative work
- Admin (email, contracts)
- Marketing
- Client meetings

**Strategy:** Track your time for two weeks. See where your energy actually goes.

**Analogy (Dancers):** Every movement in rehearsal counts—same with your hours.

**Section V: Building a Brand Without Selling Out**

**Branding is:**

- The story you tell
- The visuals you use
- The way people feel when they see/hear/experience your work

**Elements to Define:**

- Artist bio
- Mission statement
- Core values
- Signature style or medium

**Action Step:** Write a one-paragraph artist statement. Then translate that into a 2-sentence elevator pitch.

***Rule of Thumb:*** Branding isn't about logos. It's about clarity.

**Analogy (Writers):** Branding is your voice. Authenticity is the plot.

**Section VI: Managing Clients and Commissions Professionally**

**Client Process:**

1. Intake form
2. Discovery call
3. Quote or proposal
4. Contract
5. Deposit
6. Work timeline
7. Delivery
8. Final payment

**Tools to Use:**

- HoneyBook
- Bonsai
- Google Forms + Docs

**Boundaries to Set:**

- Turnaround time
- Revision limits
- Payment schedule
- Cancellation terms

**Analogy (Actors):** You don't go on set without a script. Don't start work without a contract.

**Section VII: Documenting and Archiving Your Work**

**Why It Matters:**

- For grants, gallery submissions, residencies
- For your portfolio
- For legal protection

**Systems to Use:**

- Airtable or Notion database
- Google Drive folders (year, medium, client)
- Archive both high-res files and behind-the-scenes photos

**Action Step:** Schedule a monthly "documentation day" to catalog your creations.

**Analogy (Photographers):** Your portfolio is your light meter—it tells others how to view your exposure.

**Section VIII: Planning Income Goals by Quarter or Season**

**Start With:**

- Desired monthly income
- Average project rate
- How many projects or sales you need to hit that goal

**Include:**

- Breaks
- Prep time
- Marketing push periods (holidays, launches)

**Tool:** Google Sheets or budgeting apps like YNAB

**Analogy (Filmmakers):** Think of your income plan like a production calendar—pre-pro, shooting, post. Build financial arcs into your year.

**Section IX: Outsourcing and Building a Creative Team**

**What to Outsource:**

- Bookkeeping
- Social media
- Website maintenance
- Shipping/fulfillment

**Where to Find Help:**

- Upwork
- Fiverr
- Local arts communities
- Interns from college programs

***Rule of Thumb:*** Start by outsourcing the task you procrastinate most.

**Analogy (Singers):** Think of hiring help like having backup vocals. You still lead—but the harmony supports the show.

**Section X: Final Strategy: Create Your Artist CEO Day**

***Once a month, spend 2–3 hours doing the following:***

- Review income + expenses
- Follow up on invoices
- Update your portfolio or bio
- Schedule content/marketing for next month
- Set a creative and a business goal

**Tools:**

- Notion
- Trello
- Pen + paper

**Analogy (Sculptors):** This is your studio cleanup. Every good artist needs a ritual reset.

**Conclusion: Running a Creative Business Is Still Creative Work**

You don't have to choose between the artist and the entrepreneur. You already know how to craft, iterate, experiment, refine, present, and revise. These are business skills too.

So build the schedule. Charge the rate. Protect the time. Send the invoice. Design the life.

Because treating your art like a business doesn't restrict you—it supports you.

**Your creativity is the product. Your business is the frame. And your future? That's the masterpiece.**

# Chapter 17: Business Structures for Artists

*Sole Proprietorship vs. LLC vs. S-Corp—What's Best for You?*

When you're selling prints, teaching workshops, producing performances, or licensing your work, you're not just an artist—you're running a business. And every business needs a structure.

Choosing the right structure—whether that's a sole proprietorship, LLC, or S-Corporation—can impact your taxes, your liability, your credibility, and your future opportunities. This chapter helps you understand your options so you can pick the path that supports both your creativity and your security.

**Why Structure Matters**

- Tax Implications: The IRS treats each structure differently.
- Legal Protection: Avoid personal liability.
- Professional Credibility: Boost confidence with clients and grantors.
- Access to Capital: Easier to open business bank accounts, apply for loans.

**Analogy (Photographers):** Think of your business structure like your camera body. The lens (your art) is important—but without the right frame, your work doesn't function.

**Sole Proprietorship – The Starting Point**

What It Is:

- Default business setup if you freelance without registering
- Legally, *you are* the business

Pros:

- Easiest and cheapest to set up
- Total control
- No separate tax filings

Cons:

- No legal separation between you and business
- Higher audit risk
- Personal assets at risk in lawsuits or debts

Good For:

- Artists just starting out
- Side hustle-level income
- Those testing the waters

Rule of Thumb:

- A sole prop is like an open mic—it's where you practice. Not where you stay forever.

Action Step:

- If you're starting with a sole prop, still open a separate business account.

**Limited Liability Company (LLC)**

What It Is:

- A registered legal entity that separates you from your business
- Offers liability protection while keeping tax flexibility

Pros:

- Personal asset protection
- Professional credibility
- Simple to manage compared to corporations
- Pass-through taxation

Cons:

- Filing fees (varies by state)
- Annual paperwork or franchise taxes

Good For:

- Full-time artists or growing businesses
- Artists taking commissions, hiring contractors, or doing public-facing work

Analogy (Painters):

- An LLC is your protective varnish. It doesn't change the art—but it shields it from harm.

Action Steps:

- File articles of organization with your state
- Apply for EIN at IRS.gov
- Draft an operating agreement (even if you're solo)

**S Corporation (S-Corp)**

What It Is:

- A tax status you elect as an LLC or corporation
- Allows you to split income into salary + distributions

Pros:

- Potential tax savings for high earners
- More professional structure

Cons:

- Requires payroll system
- Must pay yourself a "reasonable salary"
- More paperwork
- More complex tax filings

Good For:

- Artists consistently earning $50K+ in net income
- Creatives ready to scale with assistants, digital products, licensing, etc.

Analogy (Musicians):

- S-Corp is like a recording contract. It's for when you're ready to take things big time—but it comes with management and complexity.

Rule of Thumb:

- Don't rush into S-Corp status. It's a smart move *only if* the numbers justify it.

Action Step:

- Talk to a tax advisor before making this election. Timing matters.

**Comparing Business Structures**

Sole Proprietorship:

- Legal Protection:
- Separate Tax Filing:
- Cost to Start: Low ($)
- Best For: Starters, freelancers, beginners
- Tax Flexibility:
- Formality: Low

LLC:

- Legal Protection:
- Separate Tax Filing: (unless elected)
- Cost to Start: Medium ($$)
- Best For: Growing creative businesses
- Tax Flexibility:
- Formality: Medium

S-Corp:

- Legal Protection:
- Separate Tax Filing:
- Cost to Start: Higher ($$$)
- Best For: High-earning creatives
- Tax Flexibility: Limited once elected
- Formality: High

**Choosing What's Best for You**

Ask Yourself:

- How much do I earn annually?
- Do I want to protect personal assets?
- Do I plan to scale, hire, or license?
- Am I applying for grants or partnerships?

Strategy Moving Forward:

- Start as a sole prop
- Register as an LLC when income/visibility grows
- Elect S-Corp when income exceeds $50–75K/year consistently

Analogy (Actors):

- Your structure is like your resume layout. It evolves as your roles do.

**Tools for Managing Your Business Structure**

Registration Help:

- LegalZoom
- ZenBusiness
- IncFile

Accounting Support:

- QuickBooks Self-Employed
- Bench.co
- Wave

Payroll for S-Corp Owners:

- Gusto
- ADP
- Paychex

CRM/Contracts:

- Bonsai
- HoneyBook

**Conclusion: Structure Supports Freedom**

The best structure for your art business depends on where you are and where you're going. But don't ignore it—this is how you protect your time, your energy, your income, and your identity as a working artist.

Start simple. Grow wisely. Ask for help when needed.

Because **your art is powerful—and it deserves the safety and clarity of structure.**

# Chapter 18: Understanding Licensing, Royalties, and Usage Rights

M*onetizing Your Work Over and Over Again—Without Recreating It From Scratch*

Artists are often trained to trade time for money: paint the picture, get paid. Perform the gig, get paid. Shoot the wedding, get paid. But what if you could get paid *again*—and again—for the same work?

Licensing, royalties, and usage rights allow you to do just that.

Whether you're a photographer licensing images for magazines, a musician collecting royalties from streaming platforms, or a designer granting usage rights for a logo, these systems enable artists to turn creative assets into long-term revenue.

This chapter breaks down what these terms mean, how they work, and how to build a licensing or royalty strategy tailored to your craft. We'll use analogies, rules of thumb, pros and cons, and actionable strategies to help you protect your rights and monetize your art repeatedly.

**Section I: Definitions Made Simple**

**Licensing:** A legal agreement allowing someone else to use your work in a specific way, for a specific time, in exchange for payment.

**Royalties:** Ongoing payments you receive when your work is used, sold, or broadcast—often based on a percentage of revenue or usage.

**Usage Rights:** The specific conditions under which someone can use your work (e.g., how long, where, for what purpose).

**Analogy (Photographers):** Think of licensing as renting your camera to someone else—you still own it, but they get to use it for a while.

**Analogy (Musicians):** Royalties are like radio play: you make the song once, but get paid every time it airs.

**Section II: Types of Licensing Agreements**

**Exclusive License:**

- One client gets sole use of your work for a set period.
- Higher fee since you're giving up other opportunities.

**Non-Exclusive License:**

- You retain the right to license your work to others.
- Common for stock photography, music libraries, and digital art platforms.

**Perpetual License:**

- The license never expires—buyer can use it forever (often at a higher price).

**Limited-Term License:**

- Valid for a set time period (e.g., 1 year).

**Print or Run-Based License:**

- Used for apparel, posters, merchandise.
- You charge based on how many times the art is reproduced.

**Rule of Thumb:** Always define:

1. What rights you're selling
2. For how long

3. Where it can be used
4. For what purpose

**Section III: Royalties – The Artist's Passive Income Stream**

**Common Sources of Royalties:**

- Music (streaming, radio play, sync licensing)
- Writing (book publishing, Kindle sales, licensing to educational platforms)
- Photography (stock sites, licensing to publications)
- Licensing for TV, film, games, or ads
- Product collaborations (T-shirts, mugs, packaging design)

**Royalty Structures:**

- Fixed amount per sale
- Percentage of revenue
- Tiered royalty rates (the more they sell, the more you earn)

**Analogy (Painters):** Royalties are like creating one painting and licensing the image to be printed on canvas bags, calendars, and coffee mugs. You don't repaint every item—you monetize the original over and over.

**Section IV: Understanding Usage Rights**

**Categories of Use:**

- Commercial vs. Editorial
- Digital vs. Print
- Internal vs. External
- Worldwide vs. Regional

**Action Step:**

- Create a boilerplate usage rights form

- List categories, durations, platforms, and pricing tiers

**Analogy (Actors):** Usage rights are like performance contracts. You wouldn't perform a commercial without knowing how and where it will air.

**Section V: How to Set Licensing Prices**

**Variables to Consider:**

- Reach (local vs. national vs. global)
- Duration (1-time use vs. multi-year)
- Industry (nonprofit vs. corporate)
- Format (social media, billboard, packaging, broadcast)
- Exclusivity

**Pricing Strategies:**

- Base rate + usage fee
- Use rate calculators (Getty Images, Songtrust, or professional organizations)
- Bundle rights (e.g., 3-month digital + 1 print run)

**Rule of Thumb:** If usage is broad and long-term, price high. If it's small and short-term, offer a flexible rate.

**Section VI: Contracts, Terms, and Protecting Yourself**

**Essential Licensing Agreement Clauses:**

- Work description
- What rights are granted (and what are not)
- Duration of license
- Territory (where it can be used)
- Payment terms
- Termination clause

**Tools to Use:**

- Bonsai
- HoneyBook
- Freelancers Union contract templates

**Action Step:**

- Draft a standard licensing contract and keep editable versions by project type

**Analogy (Writers):** Licensing agreements are your publishing deal—without it, you're just handing out books for free.

**Section VII: Pros and Cons of Licensing & Royalties**

**Pros:**

- Passive income potential
- You retain ownership
- Scales your earnings without more time or labor
- Encourages international exposure

**Cons:**

- Requires legal knowledge or help
- Upfront time investment to learn
- Can be exploited if terms aren't clear
- Some platforms take large cuts

**Strategy:** Start with low-stakes licenses (like stock sites or digital downloads), then evolve to custom licensing for brands and clients.

**Section VIII: Real-World Examples by Artist Type**

**Photographers:**

- Stock image platforms (Adobe Stock, Shutterstock)
- Licensing to magazines or blogs
- Print releases for galleries

**Musicians:**

- Streaming royalties (Spotify, Apple Music)
- Sync licensing (TV/film)
- Sheet music sales

**Writers:**

- Royalties through Amazon KDP
- Licensing short stories to anthologies or podcasts
- Syndicated columns

**Visual Artists:**

- Licensing illustrations for packaging
- Royalties from art printed on apparel
- Publishing coloring books

**Filmmakers:**

- Licensing clips to documentaries
- Royalties from Vimeo on Demand or YouTube ads

**Designers:**

- Licensing logo use for different contexts
- Merch royalties (TeeSpring, Redbubble)
- Templates on Creative Market

## Section IX: Tools, Platforms, and Resources

**Music:**

- ASCAP/BMI (royalty collection)
- DistroKid, TuneCore (distribution)
- Songtrust (publishing admin)

**Photography:**

- Getty, Adobe Stock, EyeEm
- Pixieset (proofing + licensing)

**Design:**

- Creative Market, Gumroad
- Canva Pro elements library

**Writing:**

- Amazon KDP
- Substack (paid newsletters)

**Contracts & Legal:**

- The Artist's Guide to Copyright Law
- Freelancers Union contract builder

## Section X: Building a Licensing & Royalty Strategy

**Step 1:** Identify your most reusable work **Step 2:** Decide where and how it could be licensed **Step 3:** Create tiered pricing and packages **Step 4:** Set up a licensing agreement template **Step 5:** Test through low-risk channels (stock, Patreon, etc.) **Step 6:** Build relationships with licensors or buyers **Step 7:** Create marketing content around your licensing offers

**Analogy (Sculptors):** Treat each work like a mold. The mold is the original; licensing is pouring new value from it again and again.

**Conclusion: License Like a Leader, Earn Like an Entrepreneur**

You don't need to make more to earn more—you need to make smarter moves with what you've already created.

Licensing and royalties allow you to shift from constantly producing to continuously profiting. From trading hours for income to building revenue streams that run while you rest.

This is your permission slip to turn your best work into lasting income.

**Protect your rights. Price your usage. Leverage your legacy.**

# Chapter 19: Branding Yourself as an Artist

*Logos, Messaging, Platforms—How Your Brand Builds Value*

Too many artists think branding is just for corporations. But in today's world, branding is visibility. It's how you show up. It's how people remember you. And most importantly—it's how they decide whether to pay you.

Branding is not about faking it. It's about framing it. It's about presenting your work, your values, your voice, and your vibe in a way that's memorable, consistent, and trustworthy.

Whether you're a musician, painter, dancer, actor, photographer, or writer—this chapter is about owning your identity and designing your brand with purpose, pride, and profitability in mind.

**Section I: What Is an Artist Brand?**

Your brand is:

- What people say about you when you're not in the room.
- The story you tell through your visuals, your tone, and your presence.
- The emotional connection your audience feels with your work.

**Rule of Thumb:** Your brand isn't just what you do—it's how you make people feel.

**Analogy (Actors):** Your brand is your casting type. It's the first impression—and the one that books you the gig.

## Section II: Elements of a Strong Artist Brand

1. **Visual Identity:**

- Logo
- Colors
- Fonts
- Consistent visuals (photos, illustrations, thumbnails)

1. **Voice & Messaging:**

- Artist statement
- Bio
- Website/about page copy
- Social media captions

1. **Platform Presence:**

- Website or portfolio
- Social channels (Instagram, YouTube, TikTok, LinkedIn)
- Press or interviews

1. **Core Values & Mission:**

- What matters to you?
- What themes do you consistently explore?
- Who are you trying to reach?

**Analogy (Photographers):** Your brand is like a lens filter. It sets the tone and feel before the viewer even zooms in.

## Section III: Action Steps to Build Your Brand

### Step 1: Define Your Identity

- What do you want to be known for?
- What adjectives describe your style?
- What is your story?

### Step 2: Design Your Visuals

- Hire a designer or use tools like Canva or Adobe Express
- Choose 2–3 brand colors and 1–2 fonts
- Create templates for posts, proposals, and covers

### Step 3: Write Your Message

- Create a 1-paragraph bio
- Refine a 2-sentence elevator pitch
- Write your mission statement

### Step 4: Build Your Platform

- Claim your domain and build a simple site
- Pick 1–2 social platforms to show up consistently
- Start an email list (Mailchimp, ConvertKit, etc.)

### Step 5: Showcase Your Brand in Action

- Post process videos, behind-the-scenes, stories
- Share what you stand for and how you create
- Stay consistent with your tone and imagery

## Section IV: Pros and Cons of Artist Branding

### Pros:

- Easier for clients and fans to find and follow you
- Positions you for press, partnerships, and paid gigs

- Builds trust and authority
- Supports growth across platforms and income streams

**Cons:**

- Can feel like "marketing" or imposter syndrome
- Takes time to build consistency
- May evolve (which is okay!)

**Rule of Thumb:** If people can't describe your brand in 5 words, it needs refining.

**Analogy (Musicians):** Branding is your genre, your album art, your tour merch—cohesion sells.

**Section V: Examples of Artist Branding Done Right**

**Musician:**

- Consistent album visuals, retro vibe, authentic storytelling
- Speaks to mental health and healing through lyrics

**Painter:**

- Signature color palette + large format pieces
- Messaging focused on reclaiming culture and memory

**Actor:**

- Posts reels of diverse roles + clear headshot aesthetic
- Messaging: "complex female characters navigating resilience"

**Photographer:**

- Moody, cinematic portraits + behind-the-scenes footage
- Messaging: "I capture what people don't say out loud"

**Dancer:**

- Branded videos, choreography to trending music
- Messaging: "Dance as emotional storytelling"

**Section VI: Common Branding Mistakes and How to Fix Them**

**Mistake:** Using random visuals on every platform

**Fix:** Choose templates, colors, and a consistent layout

**Mistake:** Trying to appeal to everyone

**Fix:** Define your niche and ideal audience

**Mistake:** Inconsistent messaging

**Fix:** Write your brand story once, then repurpose it across bios, websites, and emails

**Mistake:** Waiting until you're "ready"

**Fix:** Brand as you grow. Authenticity matters more than perfection.

**Analogy (Writers):** You don't need the final chapter to publish a teaser. Share your journey.

**Section VII: Turning Your Brand Into Business**

**1. Your Brand Attracts Opportunities**

- Grants, residencies, partnerships

**2. Your Brand Sells Work**

- People buy what they recognize and trust

**3. Your Brand Builds Legacy**

- A body of work that feels cohesive, consistent, and memorable

**Action Step:**

- Build a "press kit" folder (bio, headshots, artist statement, logo, key links)

**Analogy (Designers):** A brand is like white space in design—it helps everything else shine.

**Section VIII: Long-Term Branding Strategy**

**Every 3 months:**

- Revisit your message, visuals, and audience engagement
- Run a personal brand audit
- Update your bio and pinned content

**Every 6 months:**

- Launch a new campaign or series
- Pitch yourself to podcasts, blogs, or publications

**Every year:**

- Redesign or refresh website
- Evaluate what content performed best
- Document your impact: testimonials, media features, case studies

**Analogy (Dancers):** Branding is like choreography—you develop the sequence over time, but you repeat the best parts often.

**Conclusion: Your Brand Is an Extension of Your Art**

Don't be afraid to own your story. Don't be afraid to be seen.

You've already built a creative identity—it's time to present it with clarity. Branding isn't about being loud—it's about being *understood.*

Craft your visuals. Clarify your voice. Choose your platforms. Share your process. Promote your purpose.

**Your brand is your business card, your stage, and your billboard—all rolled into one.**

Own it. Refine it. Let it work for you.

Because branding isn't selling out—it's showing up as the artist you were born to be.

# Chapter 20: Pricing Your Work with Confidence: Knowing Your Worth and Charging It

For far too long, artists have been handed a false dichotomy: create for the love of it, or charge for it and "sell out." That tired trope—the starving artist who lives for passion but dies broke—is not romantic, it's harmful.

In today's world, artistic talent is a business asset. Musicians are brands. Photographers are visual entrepreneurs. Writers are content creators. Designers are strategic communicators. Painters are storytellers on canvas. Knowing your worth and charging for it is not an act of ego—it's an act of financial self-respect.

This chapter is about shifting that mindset and equipping you with the knowledge, strategy, and confidence to put real value on your work. You'll learn rules of thumb, practical action steps, pricing formulas, the psychology of value, and how to balance creativity with commerce.

## Part I: Why Pricing Is So Emotional for Artists

### *1. Where the Money Shame Comes From*

Artists often grow up with messages like "art isn't a real job" or "you should just be grateful someone wants your work." Many feel conflicted between making a living and staying true to their vision. That internal battle is more about social conditioning than truth.

Artists give the world beauty, commentary, disruption, healing, and vision. But because that work is hard to quantify, people assume it's less valuable. That mindset often becomes internalized.

### *2. The Artist as a Business Owner*

Imagine a musician thinking, "I can't charge for this album—I wrote it during a breakup." Or a photographer saying, "I'll shoot your wedding for free because we're friends." What if the chef at your favorite restaurant offered meals based on how emotional they were when they cooked? Business doesn't work that way—and neither should art.

To build a sustainable creative career, you must treat your work like a business. That includes setting prices, creating contracts, negotiating, and saying no when needed.

## Part II: Rules of Thumb for Pricing Your Art

### *Rule of Thumb #1: If It Took You 10 Years to Learn, It's Not a $10 Job*

Too often, artists are paid for the "hour" they spend creating something, not the thousands of hours they spent learning the craft. A three-minute song may take 30 years of musicianship to write. A portrait photo might only take 1/250th of a second to snap—but it's 10,000 hours of technique behind the lens.

Price for mastery, not minutes.

### *Rule of Thumb #2: Don't Set Prices Based on Emotion*

You might "feel bad" charging your friend full price. You might "worry" a client will say no. But pricing based on fear or guilt will keep you broke. Base your prices on costs, experience, and market standards—not your insecurities.

### *Rule of Thumb #3: Always Include Time, Tools, and Talent in the Price*

A digital artist charging $50 for a logo may forget to factor in the cost of software, time spent revising, consultations, file formatting, and marketing. You're not just charging for the final product—you're charging for everything that made it possible.

### *Rule of Thumb #4: Raise Your Prices as You Grow*

Your pricing should evolve with your portfolio, skill level, and demand. Don't keep charging beginner rates after you've developed expert chops. Growth deserves a raise.

## Part III: Pricing Strategies for Artists of All Kinds

Let's break it down by discipline, with practical examples and analogies.

### *Photographers: From Click to Invoice*

A great analogy: Think of yourself as both the chef and the restaurant. You're preparing the meal, setting the ambiance, washing the dishes, and managing reservations.

A wedding photographer isn't just charging for eight hours of shooting. They're charging for pre-event meetings, travel, location scouting, photo editing (which can take 20+ hours), software, equipment, insurance, and time off due to weekend gigs.

Pricing tip: Create tiered packages with clear deliverables. Example: "$2,000 for 8 hours, 150 edited photos, and a digital album. Add-ons like prints, extra hours, or a second shooter can be priced separately."

### *Musicians: Notes, Nerves, and Negotiations*

A musician might get asked to play a local festival "for exposure." But exposure doesn't pay rent or replace broken strings.

What you're charging for:

- Rehearsal time
- Instrument maintenance
- Original compositions
- Equipment (amps, mics, etc.)
- Sound checks and travel
- Emotional energy and crowd engagement

Pricing tip: For gigs, use a performance fee + rider. For licensing music, price by project length, exclusivity, and where it will be used (TV, ad, film, YouTube).

### *Painters & Visual Artists: Canvas as a Business Card*

Let's say you paint a 24x36 acrylic piece and sell it for $300. Materials cost $75. You spent 12 hours painting and another 4 on framing and delivery.

Your rate ends up under $20/hour before expenses. Would a plumber, dentist, or accountant work for that rate? You shouldn't either.

Pricing tip: Use a formula. One example:

- (Hourly rate × hours worked) + materials + framing + markup for originality and style

Alternatively, some painters use:

- $ per square inch × size (e.g., $2/sq in × 864 sq in = $1,728)

### *Writers & Poets: Wordsmiths Deserve Wealth*

Writers often get paid pennies per word. But writing isn't just word count—it's ideation, research, rewriting, and polishing.

If you're a poet or author, factor in:

- Time writing and editing
- Research
- Marketing and promotion
- Speaking engagements

Pricing tip: For ghostwriting or freelance writing, charge by the hour, project, or word—but include a minimum project fee. For published books, calculate royalties, advances, and speaking fees as long-term income streams.

## Part IV: Action Steps to Price with Confidence

### *1. Know Your Numbers*

- How much do you need to make per month to survive?
- How many pieces, gigs, or services can you realistically offer?
- What are your material, time, and marketing costs?

Reverse-engineer your pricing from your life, not your feelings.

### *2. Research Your Industry*

See what artists in your medium and region are charging. Not to copy, but to understand market value. You're not trying to be the cheapest—you're aiming for fair and sustainable.

### *3. Create a Rate Card or Menu*

List your most common offerings with base prices. This helps you communicate clearly, sets expectations, and avoids awkward silence when someone says, "What do you charge?"

### *4. Learn to Say "No" Without Guilt*

If a client says, "That's too expensive," respond confidently: "I understand. I might not be the right fit for your budget, but I'm the right fit for clients who value this level of quality and detail."

Remember: not every opportunity is a good opportunity.

### *5. Practice Your Pitch*

Whether in person or over email, how you communicate your value matters. Rehearse what you'll say when someone pushes back on your price. Get comfortable with discomfort—it's part of being a professional.

## Part V: Pros and Cons of Pricing Structures

### *Hourly Pricing*

Pros:

- Easy to calculate
- Transparent for clients

Cons:

- Limits income to hours available
- Doesn't reward efficiency or expertise

Best for: consultations, lessons, coaching

### *Project-Based Pricing*

Pros:

- Aligns value with outcome
- Encourages efficiency

Cons:

- Requires accurate scoping
- Clients may push for extra work

Best for: design projects, writing gigs, commissioned art

### *Value-Based Pricing*

Pros:

- Reflects perceived value, not time
- Can lead to higher income

Cons:

- Harder to justify without strong branding
- Requires confidence and negotiation skills

Best for: high-end art, branding, or long-term partnerships

## Part VI: What Happens When You Undervalue Yourself

- You attract clients who don't respect your boundaries.
- You work longer hours for less money.
- You burn out and lose joy in your craft.
- You reinforce the lie that artists "shouldn't charge much."

The opposite is also true: when you charge confidently, you attract people who value your work, refer others, and treat you as a professional.

## Part VII: What Happens When You Price With Confidence

- You build a sustainable business.
- You can afford to reinvest in better tools, education, and rest.
- You gain respect and authority in your field.
- You inspire other artists to do the same.

Confidence in your pricing is contagious. It doesn't just uplift you—it uplifts the entire creative community.

## Part VIII: Good Strategies Moving Forward

1. Start with your **minimum viable rate**, then increase over time.
2. Offer **tiered packages** to meet different budgets without undervaluing yourself.
3. Build **passive income streams**: prints, templates, courses, merch.
4. Schedule **regular price reviews**: once a year or after every 10 clients.
5. Document **testimonials and success stories** to back up your rates.

Remember: pricing is not a one-time task. It's a living, evolving part of your business.

## Conclusion: You Are the Value

You don't have to wait for a gallery, label, publisher, or client to validate your worth. You are the value. Your work, your story, and your skill have impact.

Treat your art like a business not because you're selling out—but because you're buying in. Buying into sustainability. Buying into freedom. Buying into the belief that your creativity can feed your soul and your bank account.

Knowing your worth and charging it is not just about money—it's about respect. For your time. Your energy. Your gift.

And now, it's time the world pays you accordingly.

# Chapter 21: Social Media, Websites, and Monetization: Turning Digital Presence Into Financial Return

In the old world, artists had to wait for permission.

A record label to hear them.

A gallery to display them.

A publisher to back them.

A film studio to believe in them.

Now? The gatekeepers are gone. The internet is your platform. And with the right digital presence, your art can become your livelihood—not someday, but now.

Whether you're a musician uploading tracks to Spotify, a painter showcasing pieces on Instagram, a photographer building a portfolio site, or a dancer going viral on TikTok—your digital presence is more than a place to post. It's your storefront. It's your billboard. It's your handshake with the world.

But here's the million-dollar question: **How do you turn likes, follows, and clicks into dollars, deals, and real, repeatable income?**

This chapter is your deep dive into that answer.

## Part I: The Digital Stage – Why Every Artist Needs an Online Presence

### *The Myth: "If My Art Is Good Enough, People Will Find It."*

Wrong.

Even the most gifted artist is invisible without visibility. In today's digital economy, **you're not just creating art—you're also curating attention**.

Musicians don't just drop an album—they drop an album trailer, post reaction videos, do behind-the-scenes reels, host livestream listening parties, and build playlists.

Visual artists don't just hang a piece—they show the sketch process, canvas prep, color swatches, time-lapses, and final reveal across multiple platforms.

Social media isn't about showing off—it's about showing up.

### *Analogy: Your Website is the Gallery, Social Media is the Street Art*

Imagine a painter with a gorgeous gallery hidden in a back alley. That's your website with no traffic.

Now imagine murals on a city wall—bright, loud, in everyone's face. That's your social media. It gets attention.

You need both.

Use social media to **attract**, and your website to **convert**. Think of it like this:

- Social media = attention
- Website = conversion
- Email list = retention
- Monetization = outcome

## Part II: Rules of Thumb for Artists Online

### *Rule of Thumb #1: If You Don't Own It, You Don't Control It*

Instagram could change its algorithm tomorrow and cut your reach in half. TikTok might get banned. Platforms come and go—but your website and email list? Those are yours. Treat them like digital real estate.

Build on your land, not rented space.

### *Rule of Thumb #2: Consistency Builds Credibility*

Posting once a month won't build trust. Show up consistently. That doesn't mean posting every day—it means building rhythm and routine.

Create a content calendar. Schedule it like rehearsal.

### *Rule of Thumb #3: You Don't Need to Be Everywhere*

Better to dominate one or two platforms than spread yourself thin across five. Pick platforms that fit your medium:

- Instagram for visual artists
- YouTube for filmmakers and musicians
- TikTok for dancers and entertainers
- LinkedIn for commercial illustrators and design professionals
- Twitter/X for writers and short-form thinkers

### *Rule of Thumb #4: Social Media is a Funnel, Not a Finish Line*

Followers are not customers. A viral post doesn't pay bills. You need a path that moves people from "interested" to "invested."

That path: Awareness → Engagement → Trust → Sale.

Use social to point people to something deeper: a website, a shop, a booking page, a product, or an email list.

## Part III: Action Steps for Building an Online Presence

### *Step 1: Claim Your Name Across Platforms*

Buy your domain. Even if you're not using it yet. Grab your handle on Instagram, Twitter/X, TikTok, YouTube, etc. Even if you're not active—protect your brand.

Pro tip: Use a consistent handle if possible (@YourArtistName) for easy discovery.

### *Step 2: Build a Simple Artist Website*

Your website is your **digital HQ**. It doesn't have to be fancy—it has to be functional. Include:

- A homepage with a clear "about" and what you do
- A portfolio or gallery of your work
- A shop or booking/contact page
- An email sign-up form
- Social media links

Use platforms like Squarespace, Wix, or WordPress. If you sell art, consider Shopify or Big Cartel.

### *Step 3: Set Up a Newsletter or Email List*

Emails convert better than any other marketing method. Social media comes and goes—but email builds long-term community.

Use services like Mailchimp, ConvertKit, or Flodesk. Offer a freebie to get people to sign up—a behind-the-scenes video, a desktop wallpaper, or early access to new work.

### *Step 4: Create Content Buckets*

Don't post randomly. Create content in categories or "buckets." For example:

- Behind the scenes
- Finished work
- Process videos
- Artist thoughts/journals
- Tutorials
- Fan shoutouts or testimonials
- Announcements

If you're a musician, think: rehearsal clips, sound checks, lyrics, inspiration stories.

If you're a photographer: editing time-lapses, location scouting, gear breakdowns.

If you're a dancer: warmups, choreography breakdowns, bloopers, performances.

### *Step 5: Monetize Your Content Ecosystem*

Now we're getting to the good stuff: turning digital attention into actual dollars.

## Part IV: Monetization Methods for Artists

### *1. Direct Sales (Physical or Digital Products)*

Examples:

- Prints
- Albums

- Courses
- Zines
- Digital downloads (brush sets, presets, templates)

Artists can sell direct from their websites or via Etsy, Gumroad, or Ko-fi.

### *2. Services (Freelance Work, Commissions, Consulting)*

You can book gigs straight from DMs, but having a form or professional process builds trust.

Examples:

- Portrait sessions
- Logo design
- Music production
- Art commissions
- Creative consulting

Price with boundaries. Display starting rates. Collect deposits.

### *3. Crowdfunding and Support Platforms*

- Patreon: Subscription-based community with tiered rewards
- Buy Me a Coffee / Ko-fi: One-time support
- Kickstarter: For launching big projects
- GoFundMe: For short-term creative emergencies

Best when paired with storytelling and consistent updates.

### *4. Licensing & Merchandising*

Your art can live beyond its original format.
Examples:

- Musicians licensing songs for ads or film
- Artists licensing patterns to clothing or homeware brands
- Photographers licensing prints to stock photo libraries

Use sites like Artlist, Pond5, Society6, Redbubble, Teespring, and Printful.

### *5. Affiliate Income & Brand Collaborations*

Once you build trust with an audience, brands may pay for access.

- Musicians may get deals with gear companies
- Dancers might promote apparel or training equipment
- Writers might partner with journaling or software brands

Affiliate links earn you a cut of any sale you influence. Disclosure is legally required, but authenticity is morally required.

## Part V: Pros and Cons of Going Digital

### *Pros*

- Scalable income (sell one painting or 1,000 prints)
- Creative freedom
- Global reach
- Control over branding and voice
- Opportunities for passive income

### *Cons*

- Time-consuming content creation
- Learning curve for tech
- Audience building takes patience
- Social media burnout
- Inconsistent income if not structured

## Part VI: Good Strategy Moving Forward

1. **Pick 1-2 platforms to master.** Build community before expanding.
2. **Set up your "home base."** Website, email list, basic e-commerce.
3. **Create regular content.** Schedule time to create and engage.
4. **Offer multiple ways to support.** Free (follow, share), paid (buy, book, tip), recurring (Patreon, subscription).
5. **Learn basic business skills.** Taxes, contracts, pricing, marketing.
6. **Stay human.** Show your face. Share your journey. Let people connect with YOU, not just your product.

## Part VII: Artist Analogies to Bring It All Home

### *Photographers: Think Exposure Triangle—Shutter, Aperture, ISO*

To get a good exposure online, balance:

- Shutter (Speed = how often you post)
- Aperture (Depth = how personal/engaging your content is)
- ISO (Noise = how much you're willing to experiment)

Too much noise, you lose clarity. Too little speed, you go dark.

### *Musicians: Think of Social Media Like a Setlist*

Every post is a song. Structure your content like a performance:

- Opener = Hook (a viral idea)
- Middle = Story (your craft, your process)
- Closer = CTA (buy, book, share)

Rehearse your message. Play your hits. Don't be afraid to remix your work.

### *Actors: Think of Each Platform Like a Role*

Instagram is your romantic lead—pretty and curated.

Twitter/X is your monologue—sharp, fast, raw.

YouTube is your feature film—longform, immersive.

TikTok is your audition tape—grab attention instantly.

Play the roles that fit your story—but make sure they all lead back to your real identity.

### *Painters: Think of the Internet as a Series of Canvases*

Each platform is a different size and texture.

- Instagram = small canvas, bright colors
- YouTube = giant wall
- Website = curated solo show
- Newsletter = handwritten letter to collectors

Paint accordingly.

## Part VIII: Common Mistakes to Avoid

- Buying followers (kills engagement and trust)
- Ignoring analytics (data is feedback, not failure)
- Posting without purpose (ask: "What do I want them to do next?")
- Not having clear links (every post should point somewhere)
- Trying to go viral instead of go valuable

## Conclusion: Turn the Spotlight Into a Studio

Visibility is the first step. Monetization is the goal. But it's not just about money—it's about making your creativity sustainable.

Build your digital presence not just to be seen, but to be paid.

Your art deserves a platform. Your voice deserves an audience. And you deserve to thrive—not just survive.

# Chapter 22: Selling Your Art: Online and In-Person

## Art Fairs, Galleries, Etsy, Shopify, and Print-on-Demand

The starving artist myth has long been embedded in our culture—this belief that true creatives should struggle for years, waiting for their "big break," their moment in a prestigious gallery, a major record deal, or a call from Hollywood. But in today's world, **you can build your own gallery. You can sell your art on a blanket at a festival on Saturday and wake up Sunday to an online order from someone across the world.**

The rise of e-commerce, social platforms, and digital tools has cracked the gatekeepers wide open. You don't have to be "chosen" anymore. You can choose yourself—and build your own system for getting your art into people's hands.

This chapter explores the realities, strategies, and financial truths about selling your art both online and in-person—through galleries, fairs, websites, and print-on-demand platforms.

## Part I: Rules of Thumb for Selling Your Art

### *Rule of Thumb #1: Know Your Audience Before You Pick Your Platform*

Selling is not about shouting into a void. It's about putting your work where people who want it already are. If your art appeals to Gen Z fans of indie fashion, Etsy might be ideal. If your paintings are luxury décor, you might want galleries or curated Shopify stores.

### *Rule of Thumb #2: One Stream of Sales is Not a Strategy*

Artists who thrive financially diversify their income. Don't rely on one channel. Use art fairs to meet people, Etsy for handmade goods, Shopify for exclusive drops, and print-on-demand for scale. One piece of art can live in five places and generate five kinds of income.

### *Rule of Thumb #3: You Need a System, Not Just Sales*

Selling art isn't just about being talented—it's about systems. That means tracking inventory, packaging orders, calculating margins, communicating with buyers, and reinvesting revenue.

The same way a musician builds a tour schedule or a photographer preps a shoot list, you need a back-end that supports your front-facing creativity.

### *Rule of Thumb #4: The First Sale is Just the Start*

Don't just sell to strangers—build relationships with buyers. Your first sale should lead to a follow-up, a referral, a newsletter subscription, or a collector's discount. You're not looking for one-time buyers; you're building a base.

## Part II: In-Person Selling – The Art of Showing Up

## *A. Art Fairs and Markets*

Art fairs are the artist's version of street performing, pop-up concerts, and traveling theater—you're live, engaging, and ready to perform.

**Pros:**

- Direct feedback from real people
- Immediate cash sales
- Build local connections
- Opportunity to upsell and educate

**Cons:**

- Labor-intensive setup
- Weather, foot traffic, and sales can vary
- Booth fees, travel, and materials can eat profit
- Introverts may struggle with constant engagement

**Action Steps:**

1. Research fairs that fit your art style and pricing level.
2. Practice your booth setup in advance—make it welcoming, not cluttered.
3. Offer various price points (e.g., $5 stickers, $50 prints, $500 originals).
4. Collect emails or social follows after each sale.
5. Accept multiple payment options (Square, Venmo, Apple Pay, cash).

**Photographer analogy:** Think of art fairs like shooting street photography—you have to stay alert, interact with your environment, and adapt to light, timing, and people's reactions.

### *B. Galleries*

Galleries are the fine-dining experience of art—carefully curated, formal, and often focused on exclusivity.

**Pros:**

- Exposure to high-end collectors
- Adds prestige and credibility
- Professional presentation of your work

**Cons:**

- Commission rates are often 30%–50%
- You may have to split rights or restrict sales elsewhere
- Fewer pieces may sell, and they sell more slowly

**Action Steps:**

1. Start with local galleries and group shows—build reputation.
2. Submit professional-quality images and artist statements.
3. Understand contracts—ask about commissions, exclusivity, and payment timing.
4. Network at openings and gallery events.
5. Use galleries as part of a broader strategy—not your only sales outlet.

**Actor analogy:** Getting into a gallery is like booking a role in a stage play—it's prestigious, it can elevate your reputation, but it's not your only career move. You still need reels, gigs, and indie work to build your brand.

## Part III: Selling Online – Art That Never Sleeps

## *A. Etsy*

**Etsy** is the indie record store of online sales—quirky, personal, and full of handmade charm. It's ideal for artists who sell prints, jewelry, ceramics, small paintings, and digital downloads.

**Pros:**

- Built-in audience
- Easy to start and use
- SEO helps people find you
- Community-focused vibe

**Cons:**

- Competitive marketplace
- Transaction and listing fees
- May feel saturated or trend-driven
- Limited control over branding

**Action Steps:**

1. Invest in great product photos and tags.
2. Use SEO-friendly descriptions (use words buyers search).
3. Bundle items or offer sets to raise cart value.
4. Offer shipping upgrades, gift wrapping, and coupons to improve experience.
5. Cross-promote with social media and email to drive your own traffic.

**Musician analogy:** Selling on Etsy is like uploading to SoundCloud—easy entry, built-in audience, but you have to stand out with style, storytelling, and a unique voice.

### *B. Shopify*

Shopify is your digital flagship store. It gives you full control, analytics, and integration—ideal if you want to build a serious business.

**Pros:**

- Full branding control
- Scales well as you grow
- Add apps for upselling, email, and marketing
- Higher credibility

**Cons:**

- Monthly fee
- You drive your own traffic
- Steeper learning curve

**Action Steps:**

1. Use a clean, mobile-optimized template.
2. Set up email marketing from the start.
3. Launch with a collection, not a single item.
4. Add a blog or artist journal to connect with collectors.
5. Learn basic SEO and Facebook/Instagram ads.

**Painter analogy:** Shopify is your solo gallery exhibition—you're responsible for the lighting, signage, pricing, marketing, and ambiance—but you keep the profit and brand control.

### *C. Print-on-Demand (POD)*

POD services like Printful, Redbubble, and Society6 let you upload artwork that gets printed on products like t-shirts, mugs, canvases, and pillows—without managing inventory.

**Pros:**

- No upfront product costs
- Automated fulfillment
- Reach new audiences

**Cons:**

- Lower profit margins
- Less quality control
- Generic templates and limited customization
- Harder to build brand loyalty

**Action Steps:**

1. Choose 1–2 POD platforms to start.
2. Focus on standout designs, not quantity.
3. Promote your POD shop as part of your ecosystem—not your main brand.
4. Encourage fans to share photos of your merch.
5. Use your POD income to fund higher-end projects.

**Writer analogy:** POD is like self-publishing an eBook through Kindle—it's hands-off, scalable, and decent passive income—but doesn't replace the need for personal storytelling or brand development.

## Part IV: Pricing Strategy and Financial Discipline

### *How to Price Your Art for Each Platform*

1. **Galleries:** High-end pricing. Add 50% markup to account for commissions.
2. **Art Fairs:** Mix of high and low. Attract attention with small items, then pitch larger works.
3. **Etsy:** Competitive but profitable. Don't race to the bottom.
4. **Shopify:** Set your pricing to reflect quality. Offer bundles and memberships.
5. **POD:** Price slightly higher than default for decent margin, but stay reasonable.

**Key Financial Metrics:**

- Cost of goods sold (COGS)
- Time invested
- Shipping and packaging
- Fees and platform cuts
- Marketing expenses

**Don't forget to track:**

- Which products sell best
- Customer lifetime value
- Return rate and feedback

## Part V: Pros and Cons of Selling Platforms

Platform Pros Cons

Art Fairs

Direct cash, real feedback

Setup costs, weather, manual labor

Galleries

Prestige, high-end buyers

High commission, slow turnover

Etsy

Community, traffic, ease of use

Competition, platform fees

Shopify

Branding, customization, growth potential

Learning curve, traffic responsibility

Print-on-Demand

Passive income, no inventory

Lower margins, limited branding

## Part VI: A Balanced Strategy Going Forward

- **Start small:** Try local fairs and Etsy while building your brand online.
- **Grow intentionally:** Move into Shopify as you scale. Add galleries as prestige grows.
- **Build community:** Email, social, repeat customers matter more than one-off sales.
- **Diversify income:** Don't rely on one channel. Use multiple streams strategically.
- **Track everything:** What sells, what flops, what drains you, and what excites you.

## Part VII: Artist Analogies to Cement It All

**Photographer:**

Selling online is like running a photo studio. Each platform is a different lens. Etsy is a wide-angle—showcase everything. Shopify is your macro lens—focus on detail and polish. Art fairs are like candid shots—spontaneous, emotional, real-time.

**Actor:**

In-person selling is like live theater. You feed off energy, build relationships. Online is like film—you edit, refine, and reach bigger audiences over time. Use both mediums to build your fan base.

**Musician:**

Selling on multiple platforms is like releasing music on vinyl, Spotify, and in concert. Not everyone buys the same way—some want the digital download, others want the limited-edition vinyl.

**Painter:**

Selling in-person is plein air—live, raw, unpredictable. Selling online is like a curated studio exhibition—controlled lighting, planned layout, broad reach. Both are valid canvases for success.

## Conclusion: Selling Is Storytelling

At the end of the day, selling your art isn't just about making money—it's about **inviting someone to take a piece of your soul home**. Your story, your process, your intention—all of it adds value. Whether you're setting up under a tent at a street fair, hanging work in a gallery, or shipping a hoodie from your POD store, remember:

**You are the artist and the entrepreneur. The visionary and the vendor. The creative and the closer.**

And that balance—when mastered—turns your talent into a thriving, sustainable life.

# Chapter 23: Merchandise and Print Licensing for Visual Artists

**From Canvases to Coffee Mugs**

**INTRODUCTION**

Art doesn't have to stop at the original canvas.

In the past, selling a painting meant one person bought it and that was it. One-and-done. You created, you sold, and you started over.

But in today's digital world, one image can live in many forms:

On walls. On t-shirts. On mugs. On phone cases. On journals.

You no longer have to sell a piece of art only once.

You can sell it a hundred times—without even picking up a brush again.

This chapter will help you understand how to:

- Turn your art into merchandise
- License your art for royalties
- Create passive income from prints and products
- Protect your rights and your brand
- Build a strategy that honors your art and grows your income

## WHAT IS MERCHANDISE AND PRINT LICENSING?

**Merchandise:**

Physical products that feature your art—posters, shirts, calendars, mugs, pillows, etc.

**Print Licensing:**

You give someone permission to reproduce your art (not own it) for a fee, royalty, or contract period.

You keep ownership.

They pay to use your art in specific ways.

Example:

- You paint a sunflower piece.
- A stationery company pays you $2,000 to use it on next year's calendar.
- You keep the original and rights.
- You can still sell prints elsewhere.

**RULES OF THUMB**

**1. One Painting Can Be 100 Products**

Don't stop at the original. Think mugs, tapestries, stickers, puzzles, and more.

**2. Licensing Is Not Selling Your Soul**

You keep control. You grant *temporary use,* not ownership. Define terms in writing.

**3. POD (Print-on-Demand) Is a Launchpad, Not a Lifeboat**

Great way to start. But you'll make real income by building your brand alongside it.

**4. Quality Over Quantity**

Start with 3–5 products that fit your style. Don't flood the market with cheap, off-brand junk.

**5. Keep Your Files Organized**

High-res. Labeled. Backed up. Consistent formats. This is your digital inventory.

**6. Think Like a Storefront**

Your art is the product, but your packaging, storytelling, and presentation are your sales team.

**ACTION STEPS MOVING FORWARD**

**STEP 1: DECIDE YOUR PATH**

Choose one or more of these approaches:

- **DIY MERCH:**
- You make, print, ship, and control everything.
- More work, more profit.
- **PRINT-ON-DEMAND:**
- You upload files to a site (like Redbubble or Society6).
- They handle everything. You get a royalty.
- **LICENSING:**
- A brand or manufacturer pays you to use your art.
- You negotiate terms, royalties, or flat fees.

## STEP 2: DIGITIZE AND PREP YOUR ART

- Use a high-resolution scanner or DSLR camera
- Save in 300 DPI minimum
- Clean up files in Photoshop or Lightroom
- Save layered and flattened versions (.PSD + .JPG/.PNG)
- Use transparent backgrounds when needed
- Name files clearly (ex: "Sunflower_BlackBorder_FINAL.png")

## STEP 3: CHOOSE YOUR PLATFORMS

**Print-on-Demand Options:**

- Redbubble
- Society6
- Threadless
- InPrnt
- TeePublic
- Printful (integrates with Shopify or Etsy)
- Zazzle

**For Licensing or Commercial Reuse:**

- ArtLicensingShow.com

- Artspan
- Adobe Stock
- Direct outreach to brands
- Licensing agents

**DIY Merch Options:**

- Shopify
- Etsy
- WooCommerce
- Local print shops

## STEP 4: UNDERSTAND PAYMENT STRUCTURES

**Print-on-Demand Royalties:**
Usually 10%–20% per sale
($2–$5 profit on a $25 item)
**Flat Fee Licensing:**
One-time use. You set the price ($500+, depending on use)
**Royalty Licensing:**
You earn a percentage of each sale (usually 5%–10%)
**Hybrid Model:**
Upfront payment + royalties
Track all of it. Know your rights. Protect your work.

## STEP 5: MARKET YOUR PRODUCTS

- Don't just upload and wait—promote your merch.
- Create styled product photos
- Tell the story behind the piece
- Offer limited-edition drops
- Send to your email list
- Bundle items (print + mug + sticker = collector set)

## PROS AND CONS

**MERCHANDISE (POD or DIY)**

Pros:

- Passive income
- Repeatable revenue
- Global reach

Cons:

- POD has low margins
- You must market yourself
- Setup can be time-consuming

**LICENSING**

Pros:

- Professional reach
- Scalable
- Ongoing royalties

Cons:

- Negotiation required
- Creative limitations
- Payment may take time

**ANALOGIES FOR ARTISTS**

**Photographers:**

Merch is like stock photography. One shoot = hundreds of uses.

**Musicians:**

Merch is your version of album sales + licensing = radio plays.

**Actors:**

Your original is the stage performance. Merch is the movie—seen by more people, over and over.

**Painters:**

Think of your art as the seed. Merch is the tree. The original is the root, but the branches can bear fruit again and again.

**COMMON MISTAKES TO AVOID**

- Overloading POD platforms without a plan
- Accepting licensing terms without reading the contract
- Ignoring branding—your aesthetic matters
- Failing to market products after they go live
- Using low-res files or poorly cropped art
- Undervaluing your work—ask for what it's worth

**GOOD STRATEGY MOVING FORWARD**

- Pick 1–2 pieces of art to test on merchandise
- Choose a POD platform and upload
- Launch one product (ex: print + mug)
- Promote it on your site, socials, and email
- Track your numbers (sales, traffic, profit)
- Tweak and repeat
- Start reaching out to small brands for licensing deals
- Build a licensing portfolio with digital mockups
- Create passive merch drops quarterly
- Consider exclusive items for collectors or Patreon supporters

**FINAL THOUGHTS: YOUR ART DESERVES TO TRAVEL**

Selling one painting is great.

Selling 100 mugs with that painting? That's better.

Licensing that same piece to a home goods brand? Even better.

And you still own the original.

This is not about "selling out." It's about scaling your gift.

About reaching more people without creating more stress.

About building systems that work when you're sleeping or painting or living.

Your art deserves to be seen, felt, worn, used, loved.

From canvases to coffee mugs—this is how we build financial freedom with creative power.

# Chapter 24: Streaming, Booking, and Selling Music

## Musicians: How to Earn in Today's Streaming Economy

### INTRODUCTION

Let's cut through the noise.

You're a musician. You make sounds that heal, hype, or hold people together.

But here's the truth:

In the streaming era, you can have 10,000 monthly listeners on Spotify…

…and still not make enough for groceries.

The problem?

The traditional money-making models for musicians have collapsed or evolved.

Albums don't sell like they used to. Tours cost more.

Streaming pays fractions of pennies.

But there's good news.

Artists today are building sustainable music careers through strategy, not superstardom.

They're diversifying income, creating digital products, mastering the merch table, and turning every show into a business opportunity.

This chapter is your **financial survival guide** for making music in today's economy.

Let's get into the rules, the tools, the truths, and the traps.

## WHAT THIS CHAPTER COVERS

- Rules of thumb for modern musicians
- How to structure your income
- How streaming actually pays
- Booking smarter, not just more
- Merch, licensing, and digital products
- A strategy moving forward
- Pros and cons of each income stream
- Real-world artist analogies

## RULES OF THUMB FOR MUSICIANS

**Rule #1: Treat Streaming as a Billboard, Not a Bank Account**

Streaming is discovery, not dependable income.

Don't rely on Spotify to feed you—use it to funnel fans to your shows, merch, and mailing list.

**Rule #2: Every Song is a Seed**

That track you dropped last summer?

It can grow into licensing, sync deals, merch, samples, remixes, or NFTs.

You don't just release it once—you grow it.

**Rule #3: Live Shows = Income AND Marketing**

Gigging is still the best cash flow source for many indie artists.

But it's also a content machine, a merch opportunity, and a fan-building moment.

**Rule #4: Direct-to-Fan Wins Every Time**

Email list > social followers.

Your store > iTunes.

Your VIP club > Spotify monthly listeners.

**Rule #5: Diversify Like a Band Has Members**

A band has vocals, drums, bass, keys, and lead.

Your music career should too: streaming, live, merch, licensing, teaching, content.

## INCOME STREAMS FOR MODERN MUSICIANS

1. **Streaming Revenue (Spotify, Apple, Tidal)**
2. **Digital Sales (Bandcamp, iTunes)**
3. **Live Shows & Touring**
4. **Merchandise (Shirts, Vinyl, Posters, Stickers)**
5. **Licensing & Sync (TV, Film, Ads)**
6. **Patreon or Fan Subscriptions**
7. **Teaching & Private Lessons**
8. **Session Work or Features**
9. **YouTube Monetization**
10. **Grants, Sponsorships, and Endorsements**

You don't need all 10. But you do need at least 3–5 to stabilize income over time.

## HOW STREAMING ACTUALLY PAYS

Let's break down what 1 million Spotify streams gets you:

Average payout per stream: $0.003 to $0.005

1,000,000 streams x $0.004 = **$4,000**

That's before distributor fees and splits with collaborators.

**Conclusion: streams build audience, not wealth.**

Use them to:

- Grow social proof
- Get on booking agents' radar
- Direct fans to buy something real

**Action Step:**

Make sure your Spotify profile links to your merch store, email list, and social handles.

## BOOKING AND TOURING: STILL KING (BUT COSTLY)

**How You Get Paid:**

- Flat fee ($300–$5,000+)
- Ticket split (venue takes 20–40%)
- Tips/donations
- Guarantee + bonus for turnout

**Expenses to Watch:**

- Travel, gas, lodging
- Sound tech
- Rehearsal time
- Promotion

**Action Step:**

Always run a show budget.

Even if you make $1,000—if you spend $1,100, that's a loss.

## STRATEGIC GIGGING: THINK LIKE A TOURING ENTREPRENEUR

- Use shows to capture emails or texts (fanbase = future money)
- Sell merch at every gig (10x profit vs. streaming)
- Book shows around anchor cities—maximize draw
- Collaborate with local openers to grow audience
- Use every show to shoot content (photos, behind-the-scenes, reels)

**Musician Analogy:**

Think of every show like a pop-up shop.

Yes, you're performing—but you're also selling product, building brand, and recruiting superfans.

## MERCH: YOUR MOST PROFITABLE PRODUCT

**Best-selling items:**

- Shirts (profit margin: $10–$20 per shirt)
- Stickers (cheap and collectible)
- Vinyl or CDs (yes, they're still loved)
- Posters, lyric sheets, handwritten setlists
- Signed items = 20–50% more revenue

**DIY vs. Dropship:**

- DIY = better margin, more labor
- Dropship = lower margin, passive income

**Design tips:**

- Use your lyrics, logos, inside jokes, and artwork
- Limited-edition = urgency
- Tour-specific = memorabilia
- Include QR codes to scan for discounts or unreleased tracks

**Action Step:**

Start with one shirt, one sticker pack, and one poster.

Test. Track sales. Expand from there.

## LICENSING & SYNC DEALS: THE HIDDEN GEM

**Where to pitch:**

- Music supervisors (TV, movies, ads)
- Sync libraries (Artlist, AudioJungle, Epidemic Sound)
- Direct pitches to indie filmmakers, brands, or podcasters

**How you get paid:**

- Sync fee (one-time)
- Performance royalties (paid by BMI/ASCAP when aired)
- Backend royalties (as music continues to be used)

**Action Step:**

Register your songs with a PRO (Performance Rights Org).
Examples: ASCAP, BMI (U.S.); SOCAN (Canada); PRS (UK)

## FAN SUPPORT: PATREON, KO-FI, FAN CLUBS

**What to offer:**

- Early access to songs
- Behind-the-scenes content
- Exclusive merch or signed items
- Zoom Q&As or songwriting sessions
- Song dedications or name-in-credits

**Tiers to try:**

- $5/month = "demo club"
- $10/month = live-stream access
- $25/month = monthly merch

- $100/month = backstage pass (1-on-1 or producer credits)

**Musician Analogy:**

Think of Patreon like a record label—but the fans are the investors. They fund your art in exchange for access, not ownership.

## YOUTUBE & CONTENT MONETIZATION

YouTube is NOT just a place to post music videos.

It's your digital stage.

**What to post:**

- Lyric videos
- Performance clips
- Vlogs from the road
- "Making of the song" breakdowns
- Songwriting or gear tutorials
- Covers or mashups (copyright safe versions)

**Monetization Options:**

- YouTube Partner Program (ads)
- Channel memberships
- SuperChats on livestreams
- Sponsorships (brand deals)

**Action Step:**

Post 1 video per week. Keep it short (under 5 minutes), clear, and in your voice.

## DIGITAL PRODUCTS = PASSIVE INCOME

What you can sell digitally:

- Stems or instrumentals
- Sample packs
- Beat licenses
- Lyric books or PDF scores
- Vocal presets
- Sheet music
- Production templates
- Courses on songwriting, beat making, or music theory

**Platform options:**

- Gumroad
- Bandcamp
- Shopify
- SoundBetter
- Airbit (for beat licensing)

## TEACHING = STABLE, REPEATABLE INCOME

You don't have to be a superstar to teach music.
**You can teach:**

- Instruments (online or local)
- Production
- Vocal technique
- Songwriting workshops
- Industry tips (marketing, booking, branding)

**Ways to offer lessons:**

- Private Zoom calls
- Group classes
- Pre-recorded courses
- Local music schools

**Bonus:**

Teaching helps you sharpen your own skills while building a new fanbase—your students.

## BUILDING A STRATEGY MOVING FORWARD

**1. Audit Your Current Income**

Where is your money actually coming from now?
What's growing? What's flat? What drains energy?

**2. Pick 3 Key Areas to Develop:**

Example:

- Live performance
- Merch
- Patreon

**3. Create a Quarterly Release Plan:**

- Q1 = drop 1 single + new merch item
- Q2 = tour in 3 cities + drop acoustic EP
- Q3 = start Patreon + digital product
- Q4 = holiday merch bundle + licensing pitch blitz

**4. Track Everything:**

Use spreadsheets or platforms like ToneDen or Patreon Manager.
Know your margins. Know your top fans. Know your best-selling items.

## PROS AND CONS: MUSIC INCOME STREAMS

Income StreamProsCons

Streaming

Easy access, global exposure

Very low pay-per-stream

Live Shows

High profit, fan connection

Time-consuming, physically draining

Merch

High margins, brand-building

Requires inventory or setup

Licensing

Big money potential, passive after deal

Competitive, requires pitching

Patreon

Predictable income, fan loyalty

Requires content consistency

Teaching

Reliable, skill-building

Time-for-money trade

YouTube

Long-term brand growth

Slow to monetize

## FINAL THOUGHTS: YOU ARE THE BUSINESS

You are the brand.

You are the content.

You are the engine.

Stop waiting on a label.

Stop counting on virality.

Start building a real, diversified, creative career.

**Music is your art. Money is your amplifier.**

Use these tools to make noise that pays.

# Chapter 25: Touring, Performing, and Getting Paid as an Actor or Dancer

*Negotiating Contracts, Per Diem, and Union Considerations*

## INTRODUCTION

You booked the show.

The stage lights are on.

The choreography is tight.

The applause is loud.

But is your paycheck right?

In this chapter, we'll explore the **financial reality behind the scenes** for actors and dancers.

We'll talk about the money part of making art—contracts, compensation, expenses, and sustainability.

Because doing what you love shouldn't mean doing it for less than you're worth.

## SECTION 1: RULES OF THUMB FOR PERFORMING ARTISTS

**Rule #1**

**Applause is not a paycheck.**

If you're dancing for free or acting "for exposure," you're not building a career—you're building someone else's brand for free.

**Rule #2**

**The gig isn't real until the contract is signed.**

No paperwork? No performance.

**Rule #3**

**Touring is a business trip.**

Every city you travel to is part of your business expenses, your career network, and your financial future.

**Rule #4**

**Ask the hard questions before the first rehearsal.**

What's the pay?

What's covered?

What's not?

**Rule #5**

**If you can't explain your contract to another artist, you probably don't understand it yet.**

## SECTION 2: TYPES OF CONTRACTS

**Flat Weekly Rate**

You get paid the same every week, whether you perform 1 show or 8.

Steady, predictable—but make sure to clarify if rehearsals are included.

**Per-Performance Rate**

You get paid per show.

Higher earning potential—but no pay on dark days.

**Rehearsal + Performance Split**

Lower rate during rehearsal, higher once the show opens.

Common in longer-run contracts or union jobs.

**Non-Union Gigs**

No standard. You negotiate everything.

Could be great. Could be awful.

**Union Gigs (Equity, AGMA, SAG-AFTRA)**

Rates, hours, housing, per diem—all standardized.

But you must meet requirements and pay dues.

## SECTION 3: NEGOTIATING YOUR WORTH

**What to Ask Before Saying Yes:**

- Is this union or non-union?
- How much is the base pay?
- What's the duration?
- Are rehearsals paid?
- What's the per diem?
- Is travel reimbursed?
- Is housing included?
- Is there a merch split?
- Are there penalties or bonuses?
- Can I see the contract before I decide?

**Negotiation Tip:**

Don't demand. Ask.

Don't guess. Clarify.

Don't settle. Confirm.

## SECTION 4: UNDERSTANDING PER DIEM

**What is it?**

A daily allowance for meals and incidentals.

Not always included in pay—ask if it's separate.

**Range:**
$25–$75 per day, depending on the gig.
**How to Stretch It:**

- Grocery shop, don't eat out every meal.
- Stay hydrated—dehydration kills energy (and your budget).
- Save leftovers.
- Track every receipt.

## SECTION 5: HOUSING + TRAVEL

**Housing Questions:**

- Am I sharing a room or solo?
- Is there a kitchen or fridge?
- Is it walking distance to the venue?
- Who handles damages or deposits?

**Travel Questions:**

- Who books travel?
- Is it round-trip or one-way?
- Are checked bags covered?
- Are travel days paid?

**Pro Tip:**
ALWAYS get these answers in writing—email, text, or contract addendum.

## SECTION 6: UNION VS. NON-UNION

**Union Benefits:**

- Minimum rates

- Guaranteed breaks
- Penalties for overwork
- Health and retirement
- Legal protection
- Safer conditions

**Union Costs:**

- Must turn down some non-union work
- Annual dues
- Can take time to join
- Smaller market for newer performers

**Is Union Right for You?**

If you're consistently working professional gigs—YES.

If you're still building your resume—MAYBE wait and build credits.

## SECTION 7: BUDGETING ON TOUR

**Know Your Numbers:**

What are you actually making each week?

**Track These:**

- Gross Pay
- Per Diem
- Housing Costs (if any)
- Travel Costs (Uber, Lyft, baggage)
- Meal Costs
- Tips
- Rehearsal or overtime
- Emergencies

**Create a Road Budget:**

- Income (pay + per diem)
- Fixed Expenses (phone, rent, insurance)
- Variable Expenses (food, local travel, laundry)
- Savings (aim for 10–20%)
- Emergency Cushion (min. $300)

## SECTION 8: SAVING FOR TAXES

**If you're a 1099 contractor:**

YOU are responsible for taxes.

**Set aside:**

20%–30% of every check

(Yes, even the ones that don't feel like "real money.")

**What You Can Write Off:**

- Costumes
- Training
- Headshots
- Travel
- Agent fees
- Tech gear (lights, mics, phone)

**Keep receipts. Log mileage. File quarterly.**

## SECTION 9: LONG-TERM CAREER STRATEGY

**Don't just think about this tour.**

Think about 5 years from now.

10 years.

**Smart Moves Now:**

- Save a percentage of every check
- Contribute to a Roth IRA

- Get health insurance (Marketplace or union)
- Take care of your body (it is your business)
- Build an emergency fund
- Create a website or digital portfolio
- Stay connected with collaborators

**Stay searchable. Stay professional. Stay visible.**

## SECTION 10: PROS AND CONS OF TOURING

**PROS:**

- Get paid to do what you love
- Build resume and experience
- Travel to new cities
- Bond with castmates
- Expand your network

**CONS:**

- Can be physically exhausting
- Unpredictable schedules
- May lack long-term security
- Away from family/friends
- Can lose money if not budgeted correctly

## ANALOGIES FROM THE FIELD

**Photographer:**

Touring is like a traveling photo gig—you bring the camera, the lighting, and your vision to each new location. Every stop is both work and portfolio material.

**Musician:**

Think of a tour like a DIY record release—you rehearse, perform, pack your gear, live on the road, and sell merch to make the next trip possible.

**Painter:**

Imagine creating a mural in a new city every week. The process is similar, but the people, resources, and conditions change. You have to stay ready, flexible, and focused.

**Actor:**

Touring is a feature-length film in chapters. Each show is a scene. The road is your set. The crew is your cast. The difference? You live inside the story every night.

**Dancer:**

Every performance is choreography—but so is every paycheck. Plan the steps, watch the timing, and stay balanced so you don't fall out of rhythm financially.

## FINAL WORD: PERFORM LIKE A PRO, PLAN LIKE A CEO

Your talent got you the job.

Your discipline will keep you working.

Your financial literacy will let you thrive.

Don't leave money on the table.

Don't confuse exposure with equity.

Don't wait to be rescued by an agent, union, or director.

You are the brand.

You are the business.

You are the bank.

Own the stage.

Own the numbers.

Own your future.

# Part IV: Building Wealth as a Creative

*How Artists Create Stability, Security, and Freedom*

## INTRODUCTION

You're an artist.

You make.

You move people.

You pour meaning into the world.

But what if you could do all that—and also build wealth?

Not "get-rich-quick" wealth. Not lottery-ticket fame.

But long-term, real, resilient wealth.

Wealth that outlives your gigs.

Wealth that pays for rest, freedom, and choices.

Wealth that funds your next project without begging a patron or chasing a trend.

This chapter is about redefining wealth for creatives.

It's not about becoming a "sellout."

It's about building a strong financial foundation—without ever compromising your artistic identity.

## SECTION 1: WHAT IS WEALTH FOR AN ARTIST?

**Wealth is not about flashy cars or millions of followers.**

For a creative, wealth means:

- Freedom to choose what projects to take
- Peace of mind between contracts
- The ability to rest, heal, and restart
- Owning your time
- Leaving something behind (a body of work *and* a bank account)

**Musician Analogy:**

Think of wealth as your master recording.
Once it's laid down, it can keep generating revenue for decades.
A song that pays again and again—just like well-managed wealth.

## SECTION 2: RULES OF THUMB FOR ARTIST WEALTH

**Rule #1:**

Make money from your art.
Save money from your art.
Invest money because of your art.

**Rule #2:**

The gig pays the bills. The plan builds the wealth.

**Rule #3:**

You can't create from burnout or bankruptcy.
Money is not the enemy—it's your engine.

**Rule #4:**

Pay yourself first.
Every check. Every commission. Every show.

**Rule #5:**

You don't need to make six figures.
You need to **keep** what you make—and grow it.

## SECTION 3: BUILDING A MONEY FOUNDATION

### *Step 1: Build Your Emergency Fund*

Minimum: 3–6 months of expenses.

Ideal: 12 months (especially if your income is irregular).

**Use a separate high-yield savings account.**

Label it: "Artist Freedom Fund."

You'll use it when gigs fall through, health surprises happen, or your creative soul needs a break.

### *Step 2: Pay Off High-Interest Debt*

- Credit cards = creativity killers.
- Pay more than the minimum.
- Use the snowball (smallest first) or avalanche (highest interest first) method.

**Painter Analogy:**

Think of debt as mold on your canvas.

If you don't clean it early, it spreads—quietly eating away your art and your energy.

### *Step 3: Budget Like a Freelancer*

Your income fluctuates—so your budget must flex.

**Monthly money formula for creatives:**

- 50% = Needs (rent, food, insurance)
- 30% = Wants (gear, travel, self-care)
- 20% = Financial goals (debt, savings, investments)

**Pro tip:**

Use three bank accounts:

- Everyday checking
- Artist savings (taxes + emergencies)
- Personal freedom (vacation, sabbatical, side projects)

### *Step 4: Pay Yourself a Salary*

Even if you're self-employed.

Especially if you're self-employed.

Pick a base income to "pay" yourself monthly.

Keeps you stable. Calms your nervous system.

Helps you plan.

**Actor Analogy:**

You wouldn't improvise every line on opening night.

Don't improvise your finances either.

## SECTION 4: SAVING AND INVESTING FOR THE LONG HAUL

### *Start With a Roth IRA*

Tax-free retirement account.

You invest after-tax dollars. It grows tax-free. You withdraw it tax-free.

**Annual limit (2024):** $7,000

Even $25/month adds up.

**Dancer Analogy:**

Investing is choreography for your future self.

Every step compounds. Every movement echoes.

### *Use a SEP IRA or Solo 401(k) If You're a Business*

Self-employed with decent income? These options let you save MUCH more.

- SEP IRA: Up to 25% of income (max $66,000/year)
- Solo 401(k): Up to $66,000/year with employee/employer contributions

**Perfect for:**

- Touring musicians
- Freelance photographers
- Teaching artists
- Directors and choreographers with 1099 income

### *Learn to Love Compound Interest*

**Example:**
Invest $200/month starting at age 30.
By 60, that's over $200,000 (assuming 7% return).
**Photographer Analogy:**
It's like a long exposure shot:
Nothing seems to change at first—but if you're patient, the full picture emerges.

## SECTION 5: DIVERSIFYING INCOME STREAMS

**Your creativity is a well.**
Don't pump water into only one bucket.

### *Common Creative Income Sources:*

- Original work sales
- Commissions
- Merch
- Digital products (ebooks, templates, music packs)
- Licensing and royalties
- Teaching or workshops
- Online courses
- Speaking
- Affiliate marketing
- Passive income (investments, digital content)

**Actor Analogy:**

You're not just the star—you're also the producer, the brand, and the merch line.

Build the whole show.

## SECTION 6: PROTECTING WHAT YOU BUILD

### *Get Insured. Period.*

- Health insurance
- Equipment insurance
- Liability insurance
- Disability (if your body is your job)
- Life insurance (especially if you have a family or dependents)

### *Create an LLC or Business Entity*

Separates your personal and business assets.

Better tax treatment.

Looks more professional to clients and collaborators.

### *Have a Will and Estate Plan*

You're not too young.

You're not too broke.

You have a body of work. That's worth protecting.

## SECTION 7: THE PROS AND CONS OF BEING A CREATIVE ENTREPRENEUR

**ProsCons**

Total creative freedom

Irregular income

Flexible schedule

No employer benefits

Build your own brand

Requires discipline

Unlimited income potential

Must pay your own taxes

Scalable business models

Isolation or burnout risk

## SECTION 8: STRATEGY MOVING FORWARD

**Step 1:**

Build your Artist Emergency Fund.

**Step 2:**

Get debt-free or on a payoff plan.

**Step 3:**

Start saving 10%–20% of your income.

**Step 4:**

Open a Roth IRA or Solo 401(k).

**Step 5:**

Add a second income stream (merch, teaching, digital sales).

**Step 6:**

Get insurance + separate your business (LLC or DBA).

**Step 7:**

Schedule a money date with yourself monthly.

**Step 8:**

Think in decades—not just deadlines.

## SECTION 9: ANALOGIES THAT STICK

**Painter:**

Every brushstroke is an investment. Wealth is your full canvas—built over years, layer by layer.

**Musician:**

Think of compound interest like harmony—small notes played over time become powerful compositions.

**Actor:**

Wealth is your understudy—it shows up when you can't. Build it so you're never out of the spotlight financially.

**Photographer:**

Financial freedom is a landscape shot—it takes patience, vision, and composition.

**Dancer:**

Wealth is choreography for the rest of your life. You need balance, rhythm, and space to breathe.

# CONCLUSION: CREATE ART. BUILD WEALTH. LIVE FREE.

You don't have to choose between art and stability.

You don't have to struggle just to be considered "authentic."

You don't have to chase the next gig out of panic.

You are more than your next performance.

You are more than your next gallery show.

You are more than your last check.

Wealth gives you freedom.

It gives your art longevity.

It gives your future options.

And here's the best part:

You already have what it takes.

You know how to show up every day and practice.

You know how to push through fear and still perform.

You know how to turn ideas into emotion, story, sound, or movement.

Wealth is built with that same energy.

This isn't the end of your journey.

This is the beginning of your legacy.

# Chapter 26: Investing Basics for Artists

## Why and How to Start Investing, Even with Small Amounts

### Introduction

You're an artist.

You tell stories.

You shape emotion.

You know how to make something from nothing.

But when it comes to investing, you've probably thought:

"I don't make enough to invest."

"I don't understand the stock market."

"That's for people with suits and financial advisors."

Let's be clear. Investing is not just for the wealthy.

It's not only for people with finance degrees.

It's for you. Right now. Even if you're starting with $5.

Investing is how you take care of future-you.

It's how your money starts working while you're rehearsing, painting, writing, or sleeping.

This chapter is about showing artists that wealth isn't just for hedge fund managers. It's for choreographers.

It's for illustrators.

It's for musicians with day jobs.

It's for you.

## What is Investing?

Investing is putting your money into something with the expectation that it will grow over time.

You plant a dollar today. You grow more dollars tomorrow.

You're not just earning from your labor—you're earning from your money's labor.

That's the difference between a paycheck and a portfolio.

Your paycheck pays once.

Your portfolio pays again and again.

You can invest in many things:

Stocks

Bonds

Mutual funds

Real estate

Businesses

Even yourself

But this chapter focuses on the basics—starting with the stock market, because it's the easiest entry point for most artists.

## Why Investing Matters (Especially for Artists)

As artists, we often have income that's inconsistent.

Some months are feast. Others are famine.

A traditional 9-to-5 may come with a retirement plan.

But for many creatives, there's no employer matching, no automatic savings, no pension.

That means we must build wealth on purpose.

Here's why investing is essential:

It builds freedom

It creates options

It offers protection during slow months

It gives you power to say no to bad gigs

It supports rest and retirement

It allows you to make long-term decisions, not just survive the short term

Think of it like a stage manager. You're the performer. But investing helps everything behind the scenes run smoothly—even when you're offstage.

## Rules of Thumb for Artist-Investing

Start small, stay consistent

Investing is not about huge lump sums. It's about building habits. Even $25 a month makes a difference.

Don't try to time the market

Focus on time *in* the market. Investing works because you stay in it, not because you predict it.

Don't invest money you'll need next month

Invest with long-term goals in mind—money you don't need for at least 3 to 5 years.

Diversify

Don't put all your dollars into one stock. Spread your investments out so one bad month doesn't wreck your entire plan.

Keep fees low

Choose low-cost index funds or ETFs. Avoid "hot stock tips" and high-fee brokers.

Stay the course

Markets rise and fall. Don't panic. Artists know this—it's just like creative energy. Sometimes it flows, sometimes it dips. But it always comes back.

## Investing vs. Saving

Saving is short-term. It's for next month's rent or emergencies.

Investing is long-term. It's for next year's sabbatical. Your retirement. Your future home.

Both are important, but they serve different purposes.

Your savings is your cushion.

Your investments are your catapult.

## How to Start Investing (Even with Small Amounts)

Step one: Get clear on your goals

What are you investing for?

To stop living paycheck to paycheck?

To take a break from performing?

To retire early?

To support your art without burning out?

Step two: Set up a basic emergency fund first

Aim for $500 to $1,000 to start.

Eventually, build 3–6 months of expenses.

This protects you from needing to pull out investments early.

Step three: Open an investment account

Start with a Roth IRA if you're eligible. It's a retirement account you fund with after-tax money.

Why artists love the Roth IRA: You can invest small amounts

Your money grows tax-free

You can withdraw contributions (not earnings) without penalty

You have total control—unlike 401(k)s through a boss

You can open a Roth IRA at platforms like Fidelity, Schwab, or Vanguard.

You can also use apps like Betterment, SoFi, or M1 Finance to start with just $10 or $25.

Step four: Choose simple, low-cost investments

Index funds: They track the entire stock market or large slices of it. They're simple, reliable, and historically strong performers.

ETFs (Exchange-Traded Funds): Like index funds, but they trade like stocks. Easy to buy and sell.

Avoid stock picking—especially early on. It's like choosing one audition in a city you've never been to. You don't have enough information yet.

Step five: Automate your investing

Set up automatic transfers—even $10 a week helps.

This builds momentum and removes emotion.

You'll be investing while choreographing, painting, or writing.

## Artist Analogies: What Investing Feels Like

For a photographer:

It's like long-exposure photography. You don't see the image right away, but with enough time, light, and patience—you create something stunning.

For a dancer:

It's like training your body. One class won't change much. But daily, consistent movement transforms you over time.

For a writer:

It's like building a manuscript. Word by word, page by page. It doesn't feel big until it is.

For a musician:

It's like songwriting. Sometimes messy. Sometimes boring. But eventually, it becomes a symphony.

## Pros and Cons of Investing

Pros: Your money works while you sleep

Compound interest helps you grow wealth faster than saving

Investing builds long-term freedom

You can start with small amounts

You don't have to be perfect—you just have to be consistent

Cons: Markets can go up and down

You must wait years to see full results

It takes discipline not to cash out early

There's risk—but with education and diversification, it's manageable

## Mistakes Artists Make When Investing

Waiting too long to start

Thinking you need thousands

Listening to hype instead of doing research

Freaking out when the market dips

Thinking investing is only for retirement

Trying to "time the market" or beat it

The truth is:

The best time to start was yesterday.

The second-best time is today.

## A Good Strategy Moving Forward

Start with $25 or $50

Open a Roth IRA

Choose a low-cost index fund

Set up auto-contributions

Ignore the headlines

Check in once a quarter—not every day

Add more as your income grows

Let it compound quietly

Don't stop—even if you hit a slow month

Celebrate your progress. You're building wealth.

You don't need to be perfect.

You just need to be consistent.

## Thinking Like an Investor (Not Just a Creator)

As an artist, you already know how to:

Play the long game

Handle risk

Invest time before results

Trust your intuition

Create from limited resources

That's exactly what investing is about.

So instead of thinking: "I'm an artist—I don't know how to invest."

Think: "I'm an artist—I already know how to build something over time."

You're not behind.

You're just beginning.

And that beginning could turn into something beautiful.

## Closing Thoughts

Investing is how artists create freedom.

It's not the opposite of creativity—it's what funds it.

It's not selling out—it's building up.

It's not boring—it's empowering.

You already believe in the process.

You know how to create beauty with patience and practice.

Now, let your money do the same.

# Chapter 27: Retirement Planning for Artists – IRAs, Roth IRAs, and Solo 401(k)s

Most artists are so focused on the next commission, show, gig, or grant that they rarely pause to think 30 or 40 years down the road. But the truth is, artists need retirement plans just as much as—if not more than—those in traditional careers. Without employer-sponsored pensions or 401(k) matches, it's up to you to build your own safety net. The good news? You have options.

In this chapter, we'll explore retirement savings tools available to self-employed creatives—including IRAs, Roth IRAs, and Solo 401(k)s—and how to use them to build a retirement that gives you both freedom and dignity.

## Why Artists Need to Think About Retirement

- You may not have access to employer-sponsored plans
- Your income may be inconsistent year-to-year
- You're responsible for your own future
- Compound interest needs time to work—starting early is key

Retirement isn't about giving up your art—it's about giving yourself the choice to keep creating without financial stress.

## Traditional IRA

### *What It Is:*

An Individual Retirement Account (IRA) that lets you save for retirement with pre-tax dollars.

### *Key Benefits:*

- Contributions may be tax-deductible
- Grows tax-deferred until withdrawal
- Available to anyone with earned income
- Contribution limit for 2025: $6,500 (or $7,500 if age 50+)

### *Consider If:*

- You expect to be in a lower tax bracket in retirement
- You want a tax deduction now

## Roth IRA

### *What It Is:*

A retirement account funded with after-tax dollars. You don't get a deduction now—but your money grows **tax-free**, and withdrawals in retirement are also tax-free.

### *Key Benefits:*

- Tax-free growth and withdrawals
- Contributions (not earnings) can be withdrawn at any time
- Income limits apply (check IRS guidelines)

### *Consider If:*

- You're early in your career or in a low tax bracket
- You want flexibility without tax surprises in retirement

## Solo 401(k)

### *What It Is:*

Also called an individual 401(k), this is for self-employed individuals with no full-time employees (other than a spouse).

### *Key Benefits:*

- High contribution limits: up to $66,000 in 2025 (combined employee and employer contribution)
- Can include Roth and Traditional options
- Can take a loan from it (with restrictions)

### *Consider If:*

- You earn substantial income from your art
- You want to save aggressively for retirement
- You don't have employees

## SEP IRA (Bonus Option)

### *What It Is:*

A Simplified Employee Pension plan for self-employed people.

### *Key Benefits:*

- Contribution limit up to 25% of income or $66,000 (2025)
- Easy to set up and maintain
- Lower fees than Solo 401(k)

### *Consider If:*

- You want flexibility and simplicity
- You don't need Roth features or loans

## Choosing the Right Plan for You

ScenarioBest Option

You're just getting started and earning under $150K

Roth IRA

You want tax deductions now

Traditional IRA or SEP IRA

You earn a lot and want to max out savings

Solo 401(k)

You want simplicity without complex setup

SEP IRA

## Tips to Maximize Your Retirement Savings as an Artist

- **Automate contributions:** Set up monthly transfers, even if small
- **Increase with income:** When you have a strong year, bump up savings
- **Stay invested:** Don't pull money out unless it's a true emergency
- **Rebalance annually:** Make sure your asset mix aligns with your age and goals
- **Track fees:** Choose low-cost index funds or ETFs to reduce expenses

## Final Thoughts

You may never fully "retire" in the traditional sense—and that's okay. Many artists create well into their later years. But retirement planning isn't about stopping—it's about creating from a place of freedom, not fear.

The earlier you start—even with $50 a month—the more power you give your future self. Your art deserves longevity. So does your financial life.

Make retirement part of your artist business plan. It's not an afterthought—it's your future masterpiece.

# Chapter 28: Real Estate for Artists – Should You Rent, Buy, or Studio-Share?

Where you live and work as an artist isn't just a financial decision—it's a creative one. Real estate choices impact your mental space, your inspiration, your opportunities, and your long-term sustainability.

So how do you decide whether to rent, buy, or studio-share?

Let's break it down.

## Renting

**Pros:**

- Lower upfront costs
- Flexibility to relocate
- No responsibility for maintenance or repairs
- Good for short-term or transitional periods

**Cons:**

- No equity built
- Subject to rent increases
- Limited ability to personalize space

- No long-term security

**Best for:**

- Emerging artists
- Artists with inconsistent income
- Creatives who value mobility over permanence

## Buying

**Pros:**

- Builds equity over time
- Freedom to customize your space
- Predictable monthly payments (with fixed mortgage)
- Can potentially generate rental income

**Cons:**

- High upfront costs (down payment, closing fees)
- You're responsible for all upkeep and repairs
- Less flexibility to move
- Market risk if property value drops

**Best for:**

- Artists with stable income
- Long-term location commitment
- Those who want to combine home + studio

## Studio-Sharing

**Pros:**

- Lower cost than renting solo
- Access to shared tools and equipment
- Built-in community
- Encourages collaboration and creativity

**Cons:**

- Less privacy
- May involve schedule conflicts
- Potential for personality clashes
- Shared responsibility for space rules and cleanliness

**Best for:**

- Artists who thrive around others
- Part-time creators
- Those seeking creative community

## Buying a Live/Work Space

**What to Know:**

- Combines living space and studio in one property
- Look for spaces zoned for residential and commercial use
- Can allow you to deduct a portion of your housing costs as a business expense

**Consider:**

- Local zoning laws
- Business insurance needs
- Noise, ventilation, and safety compliance

## Rent vs. Buy: Financial Snapshot

**Rent:**

- Lower upfront cost
- Flexibility
- No maintenance
- No equity

**Buy:**

- Higher upfront cost
- Long-term investment
- Full control
- Ongoing responsibility

## Artist Real Estate Tips

- Know your budget—especially with variable income
- Keep 3–6 months of emergency funds before buying
- Use a rent vs. buy calculator to model scenarios
- Save receipts and records if you claim part of your home for business
- Consider artist housing grants or residencies

- Don't buy before you're ready just because it feels like the "adult" move

## Final Thoughts

Real estate decisions are both personal and practical. Choose what works for your lifestyle, your creative rhythm, and your financial situation.

The best space is the one that supports your art and your well-being—not just your image.

You can always level up later. But for now, choose wisely, spend mindfully, and make sure your space is helping you build a life—and a legacy—you love.

# Chapter 29: Understanding Risk and Insurance – Health, Liability, and Income Protection

As an artist, your creativity is your career—but what protects your ability to keep creating?

Insurance might not be glamorous, but it's essential. One accident, illness, or legal issue can disrupt everything you've built. Whether you're a painter, musician, dancer, or designer, understanding your risks—and how to insure against them—is a key part of building a sustainable, professional creative life.

## Why Insurance Matters for Artists

- Your body may be your instrument.
- Your studio or equipment may be expensive.
- Your income may be irregular.
- You may work gigs or freelance with no employer coverage.

Without proper protection, a medical emergency, lawsuit, or theft could derail your finances—and your future.

## Health Insurance

**What It Covers:**

- Doctor visits
- Surgeries and hospital stays
- Prescriptions
- Mental health services

**Why It's Critical:**

- One accident or illness can cost tens of thousands of dollars
- Many artist careers depend on physical health and mobility

**Options:**

- Marketplace/ACA plans (healthcare.gov)
- Medicaid (if income-eligible)
- Health insurance through a spouse or part-time job
- Freelancers Union or artist-specific co-ops

**Tips:**

- Choose a plan with a reasonable deductible and network in your area
- Consider adding dental and vision if not included
- Use a Health Savings Account (HSA) if eligible

## Disability Insurance

**What It Covers:**

- Replaces a portion of your income if you can't work due to illness or injury

**Why It's Critical:**

- If you rely on your hands, voice, body, or presence to earn—you're at risk
- Self-employed artists typically have no safety net

**Options:**

- Individual long-term disability policies
- Short-term policies for immediate needs
- Riders that cater to creatives (e.g. loss of voice, fine motor function)

**Tips:**

- Make sure your policy covers *own occupation*—not just any job
- Apply while you're young and healthy for lower premiums

## Liability Insurance

**What It Covers:**

- Legal and financial protection if someone sues you
- Injuries that happen in your studio or at your event
- Accusations of copyright infringement or professional errors

**Why It's Critical:**

- If you exhibit, perform, or interact with the public—you're exposed to risk
- One lawsuit could bankrupt your business

**Options:**

- General liability (for physical events and public spaces)
- Professional liability (for design work, consulting, teaching)
- Product liability (if you sell items)

**Tips:**

- If you teach workshops or do public events, ask about one-day or event coverage
- Some organizations (like Fractured Atlas) offer artist-specific liability insurance

## Property Insurance

**What It Covers:**

- Loss or damage to your studio, tools, instruments, art, or equipment

**Why It's Critical:**

- Your tools are your livelihood
- Homeowners or renters insurance may not cover business assets

**Options:**

- Business property insurance
- Add a rider to your home/renters policy
- Inland marine insurance for items that move with you

**Tips:**

- Keep a digital inventory with receipts and photos
- Back up your digital work regularly and insure hard drives or servers

## Income Protection and Emergency Planning

**Set up a safety net:**

- Emergency fund: 3–6 months of expenses
- Passive income streams: licensing, prints, teaching online
- Business continuity plan: what happens if you're out for 2–6 months?

**Insurance Can't Prevent Risk—But It Can Soften the Blow**

- Think of insurance like a backup plan
- You hope you won't need it—but you'll be glad it's there if you do

## Final Thoughts

Creativity is powerful—but it's not invincible. A smart artist prepares for the unexpected by protecting their health, their gear, their income, and their legal exposure.

You don't need to insure everything all at once. Start with your biggest risks, and build from there.

Because the best investment you can make in your career—is protecting the one person who creates it.

You.

# Chapter 30: Side Hustles and Passive Income Streams for Artists

Being a full-time artist doesn't mean you have to rely on one stream of income—or even one type of work. Diversifying your earnings through side hustles and passive income can provide stability, unlock new creative opportunities, and protect you during slow seasons.

This chapter explores smart, artist-friendly ways to generate extra cash without selling out or sacrificing your primary passion.

## Why You Need More Than One Income Stream

- Art sales can be seasonal and unpredictable
- Life expenses don't stop during creative dry spells
- Multiple streams mean more freedom and less pressure
- Some income can be made while you sleep or travel

## What Is a Side Hustle?

A side hustle is any job or service you take on outside your main creative work to earn extra income.

**Characteristics:**

- Usually active income (you trade time for money)
- Flexible and often part-time

- Can leverage your existing skills or explore new ones

## Side Hustle Ideas for Artists

### 1. Teaching Art Classes

- Local workshops or online platforms (e.g. Skillshare, Udemy)
- Can be group sessions or 1-on-1 coaching

### 2. Freelance Design Work

- Logos, album art, book covers, etc.
- Market through sites like Fiverr, Upwork, or direct outreach

### 3. Creative Gigs

- Photography, videography, makeup artistry, mural painting
- Partner with local businesses, venues, or events

### 4. Selling Merchandise

- T-shirts, tote bags, stickers, or zines
- Use print-on-demand services (e.g. Printful, Redbubble)

### 5. Social Media Management or Content Creation

- Help brands or nonprofits build their visual identity

### 6. Art-Adjacent Roles

- Gallery assistant, museum educator, art installer

## What Is Passive Income?

Passive income is money earned with little to no ongoing effort once the initial work is done.

**Examples:**

- Licensing your work
- Selling prints or digital downloads
- Royalties from music, books, or patterns
- Ad revenue from YouTube or a monetized blog
- Affiliate marketing

## Passive Income Ideas for Artists

**1. Sell Digital Downloads**

- Art prints, coloring pages, clip art, design templates
- Platforms: Etsy, Gumroad, Creative Market

**2. License Your Art**

- For products, apparel, book covers, greeting cards
- Use licensing agencies or platforms like Society6, Spoonflower

**3. Write a Book or eBook**

- Share your process, techniques, or art journey
- Self-publish on Amazon Kindle or sell PDFs

**4. Launch a Patreon or Subscription Model**

- Offer exclusive content to paying fans

**5. Start a Monetized YouTube Channel**

- Teach, vlog, review products, share time-lapses

**6. Create an Online Course**

- Platforms like Teachable or Thinkific

## Balancing Side Hustles With Your Core Creative Work

- Choose income streams that complement your artistic identity
- Batch similar tasks together to stay efficient
- Set boundaries so the side hustle doesn't drain your creative energy
- Use extra income to fund your main artistic projects

## Things to Watch Out For

- Don't burn out—choose 1–2 manageable streams to start
- Be mindful of taxes (track all income and expenses)
- Protect your intellectual property (use contracts and licenses)

## Final Thoughts

Side hustles aren't about distraction—they're about *protection* and *possibility.*

They give you breathing room. They give you options. They help you fund your vision without relying entirely on sales or grants.

And passive income? That's the long-term strategy for earning while you rest, reflect, or work on your next big piece.

Your art is the core. These streams are the scaffolding. Build them with intention, and you'll create not just a living—but a life that lasts.

# Chapter 31: Collaborations, Collectives, and Business Partnerships

Art doesn't always have to be a solo mission. Collaborating with others—whether informally, in a collective, or through a formal business partnership—can amplify your reach, increase income, spark new ideas, and create lasting impact.

But successful partnerships require clarity, communication, and contracts.

In this chapter, we'll explore how artists can team up effectively—creatively and financially.

## Why Collaborate?

- Combine strengths and skills
- Share audiences and visibility
- Split costs and labor
- Take on bigger projects
- Fight isolation and creative burnout

Collaboration is not just about making something together—it's about building something greater than what you could have done alone.

## Forms of Collaboration

**1. One-Off Creative Collaborations**

- Joint murals, exhibits, installations
- Co-hosting workshops or performances
- Cross-discipline projects (e.g. musician + visual artist)

**2. Artist Collectives**

- A group of artists who support each other professionally and/or financially
- May share studio space, tools, promotion, or exhibition costs

**3. Business Partnerships**

- Two or more people co-owning a business (e.g. design studio, media brand, artist-run space)
- Legally formalized with agreements on ownership, profits, and decision-making

## Pros and Cons of Collaboration

**Pros:**

- Shared resources
- Increased energy and accountability
- Expanded network
- New creative sparks

**Cons:**

- Conflicting visions or work styles
- Uneven work distribution
- Money and credit disputes
- Emotional strain if roles aren't clear

## Keys to Successful Collaborations

**1. Define Roles Clearly**

- Who's responsible for what?
- Who handles money, promotion, logistics, etc.?

**2. Talk Money Early**

- How will income be split?
- Who covers upfront costs?
- What if one person brings more resources or followers?

**3. Use Written Agreements**

- Even for friends—especially for friends
- Outline scope, timelines, payments, ownership, and exit plans
- Consider using templates or legal services (like Rocket Lawyer or LegalZoom)

**4. Protect Your Intellectual Property**

- Clarify who owns what in joint projects
- Use licensing or co-authorship where applicable

**5. Communicate Openly and Often**

- Schedule check-ins
- Address tensions before they escalate
- Be flexible—but not at the cost of your boundaries

## Starting or Joining a Collective

**Things to Consider:**

- What's the mission or shared goal?
- Will it be informal or legally structured (LLC, co-op, nonprofit)?
- Will there be shared dues or financial contributions?
- What's the onboarding and exit process?

**Examples of Collective Benefits:**

- Group shows
- Bulk supply orders
- Pooled grant applications
- Shared workspace
- Mental and emotional support

## Business Partnerships – A More Formal Path

If you're starting a company with another creative, it's vital to:

- Create an operating agreement
- Decide on equity (50/50 isn't always fair)
- Choose a legal structure (LLC, S-Corp, etc.)
- Agree on decision-making processes and dispute resolution

**Ask These Questions Before Forming a Business Partnership:**

- Do we have the same work ethic?
- Do we share values around money, risk, and growth?
- How will we handle conflict?
- What happens if one of us wants out?

## Final Thoughts

The right collaboration can elevate your career, expand your skills, and introduce you to new audiences.

But the key word is **right**.

Collaborate with clarity. Partner with purpose. Put everything in writing.

When done well, working together isn't just more fun—it's more powerful.

You don't have to do this alone. But you do need to do it smart.

# Chapter 32: How to Read Investment Statements and Track Progress

Investing isn't just about putting money in and hoping for the best. To build wealth over time, you need to understand where your money is, how it's performing, and what adjustments—if any—should be made. In this chapter, you'll learn how to read your investment statements, track your portfolio's progress, and make informed decisions along the way.

## Why This Matters for Artists

- You may not have a retirement plan through an employer
- Investing can be a major part of your long-term financial stability
- Understanding your statements empowers you to stay in control

## What to Look for on an Investment Statement

Most brokerage accounts, IRAs, and 401(k)s send out monthly or quarterly statements. Here's how to read them:

### *1. Account Summary*

- **Beginning Balance:** What your account was worth at the start of the period
- **Contributions/Deposits:** Any new money you added

- **Withdrawals:** Any money you took out
- **Ending Balance:** Your total after growth/losses and deposits/withdrawals

## *2. Portfolio Holdings*

- **List of investments you own** (stocks, funds, bonds, etc.)
- **Number of shares held**
- **Price per share**
- **Total market value** (what your holding is worth now)

## *3. Performance Overview*

- **Change in account value over time**
- **Rate of return for the period** (monthly, quarterly, or annually)
- **Dividends earned or reinvested**

## *4. Asset Allocation*

- Shows how your money is divided among different investment types:
- Stocks
- Bonds
- Cash
- Mutual Funds/ETFs
- Alternative investments

A diversified allocation is key to managing risk.

## *5. Fees and Charges*

- Review any transaction fees, advisory fees, or fund expenses
- Understand how much you're paying—and whether it's worth it

## Tracking Your Progress

### *Set Benchmarks*

- Define your personal goals (e.g. retire at 65 with $500K)
- Compare your current trajectory against where you want to be

### *Use Investment Apps*

- Tools like Personal Capital, Empower, or Mint can help visualize your progress

### *Check Quarterly, Not Daily*

- Watching daily market changes leads to stress and poor decisions
- Review statements once every 3 months to evaluate performance calmly

### *Track Contributions*

- Make sure all scheduled transfers are happening
- Increase your contributions as your income grows

## How to Tell If You're on Track

Ask yourself:

- Is my portfolio growing over time?
- Am I consistently adding to it?
- Am I diversified across asset types?
- Are my fees low and reasonable?
- Do I understand the types of investments I own?

If the answer is "no" to any of the above, consider:

- Rebalancing your portfolio
- Adjusting contributions
- Consulting with a financial advisor

## Common Mistakes to Avoid

- Obsessing over short-term performance
- Ignoring fees
- Holding too much cash (not keeping up with inflation)
- Not checking statements at all
- Overreacting to market news

## Final Thoughts

You don't need to be a Wall Street wizard to manage your investments—you just need to stay engaged, stay consistent, and understand what you're looking at.

Read your statements like you'd read a gallery review or concert contract—with care, attention, and your long-term goals in mind.

It's your money. Your freedom. Your future.

Stay informed. Stay in control. And keep investing in what matters most—you.

# Part V: Legal and Financial Protection – Safeguarding Your Art, Income, and Future

This section empowers artists to go beyond creativity and take control of the practical side of their careers. From choosing the right insurance to protecting intellectual property and preparing for the unexpected, Part V offers clear guidance on how to build a secure, resilient foundation that sustains your art and your life.

You'll learn how to:

- Insure your health, income, tools, and studio space
- Protect your legal rights with contracts and copyright knowledge
- Navigate housing and real estate choices as a creative professional
- Understand and manage financial risks
- Diversify your income to weather slow seasons
- Build partnerships, collectives, and collaborations that last
- Monitor your investments and stay financially confident

Whether you're just starting out or expanding your creative business, this section is your financial safety net. Because true artistic freedom comes when you're protected—personally, professionally, and financially.

# Chapter 33: Contracts 101 – What to Look For Before You Sign Anything

Contracts aren't just paperwork—they're protection. They spell out expectations, timelines, payments, rights, and responsibilities. As an artist, you might be asked to sign contracts for gallery shows, freelance gigs, licensing deals, collaborations, performances, and more.

This chapter gives you the tools to read, understand, and negotiate contracts with confidence.

## Why Contracts Matter

- They create legal clarity between you and the other party
- They protect your intellectual property and income
- They help avoid misunderstandings and disputes

Whether it's for $100 or $10,000, **always get it in writing.**

## Common Types of Contracts Artists Encounter

- Commission agreements
- Licensing agreements
- Gallery consignment contracts
- Freelance work agreements
- Collaboration agreements

- Performance or teaching contracts

## Key Things to Look For in Any Contract

### *1. Parties Involved*

- Make sure your full legal name or business name is used correctly
- Confirm the identity and authority of the person you're contracting with

### *2. Scope of Work*

- What exactly are you being hired to do?
- What's included—and what's not?
- Define deliverables, timelines, and milestones

### *3. Payment Terms*

- How much will you be paid?
- When will payment be made—upfront, on delivery, in installments?
- Will there be penalties for late payment?

### *4. Intellectual Property Rights*

- Who owns the final work?
- Can they reproduce, modify, or resell your work?
- Are you granting a license (temporary use) or transferring ownership?

### *5. Revisions and Changes*

- How many revisions are included?
- What happens if the client changes their mind halfway through?

### *6. Termination Clause*

- What happens if the project is canceled?
- Will you still get partial payment for work completed?

### *7. Liability and Indemnity*

- Are you responsible if something goes wrong?
- Make sure you're not unfairly taking on legal risk

### *8. Deadlines and Delivery*

- Be clear on due dates—and penalties for missing them (on either side)
- Specify format of delivery (digital files, physical prints, etc.)

## Red Flags to Watch Out For

- Vague language or unclear scope
- No timeline or payment schedule
- You give up all rights without compensation
- "Work for hire" language without clarification
- The other party refuses to put anything in writing

## Negotiating Tips for Artists

- Don't be afraid to ask questions—it shows professionalism
- Suggest changes in writing (email is fine)
- Use friendly but firm language (e.g. "To clarify, I'd like to...")
- If you're unsure, ask for time to review or consult a legal advisor

## Templates and Tools

- Use contract templates from trusted sources (e.g. Freelancers Union, Volunteer Lawyers for the Arts)
- Consider platforms like Bonsai, AND CO, or Hello Bonsai
- For complex deals, consult a legal expert or entertainment lawyer

## Final Thoughts

Your creative work deserves protection. Contracts help ensure that your time, talent, and rights are respected.

Don't let legal language intimidate you. Learn it. Use it. Protect your power.

Every time you put pen to paper—or stylus to screen—your work matters. So does your ability to defend it.

Read everything. Ask questions. And never sign something you don't fully understand.

# Chapter 34: Protecting Your Intellectual Property

Your ideas, your creations, your style—they're all part of your intellectual property (IP). Whether you're a visual artist, writer, musician, filmmaker, or designer, your work has value. And just like money or physical assets, it needs to be protected.

This chapter breaks down the basics of IP for artists and shows you how to defend your work from misuse, theft, or exploitation.

## What Is Intellectual Property?

Intellectual property refers to creations of the mind. For artists, this includes:

- Paintings, drawings, and sculptures
- Photographs
- Songs, beats, and lyrics
- Choreography and performance pieces
- Graphic designs and illustrations
- Written works like books, scripts, or poems

## Types of Intellectual Property Protection

### *1. Copyright*

**What it protects:** Original creative works (music, art, writing, film, etc.)

**Automatic protection:** In the U.S., your work is protected by copyright the moment it's created and fixed in a tangible form (like a file or canvas).

**Why register it:**

- Makes it easier to prove ownership
- Allows you to sue for damages
- Required for licensing or legal enforcement

**Where to register:**

- U.S. Copyright Office (www.copyright.gov)

### *2. Trademark*

**What it protects:** Names, logos, slogans, or branding that identifies your work or business

**Why it matters:**

- Prevents others from using your brand name or logo
- Adds value to your business identity

**Where to register:**

- U.S. Patent and Trademark Office (www.uspto.gov)

### *3. Trade Secret*

**What it protects:** Confidential processes, recipes, or methods (more relevant for creative businesses than individual artworks)

### *4. Patent*

**What it protects:** Inventions or unique physical product designs (rare for most artists but relevant for those creating tools, devices, or software)

## Common IP Scenarios for Artists

- Someone reposts your art without credit
- A company uses your design on merchandise without permission
- Your music is used in a commercial or video without a license
- Another artist mimics your exact style and claims originality

## How to Protect Your Work

### *Use Watermarks or Metadata*

- Especially for images shared online
- Add contact info or copyright notices in file properties

### *Add a Copyright Notice*

- Format: © [Your Name] [Year]
- Example: © Jordan Rivers 2025

### *Keep Proof of Creation*

- Save original files, sketches, drafts, or timestamps
- Email yourself versions to create a date trail

### *Register Key Works*

- If you're selling, licensing, or publishing—register your copyright
- Consider registering series or portfolios together to save money

### *Use Contracts for Collaborations*

- Define who owns what
- Decide how profits, licenses, and rights will be shared

## What to Do If Your Work Is Stolen

1. **Document the violation** (screenshots, links, time/date)
2. **Reach out** politely and request removal or payment
3. **File a DMCA takedown notice** (for online infringement)
4. **Consult a legal expert** if damage is significant or unresolved

## Licensing Your Work: Turn IP Into Income

Licensing allows others to use your work—for a fee—without giving up ownership.

You can license:

- Artwork for use on products
- Music for film or ads
- Text for websites or books

**Always use a written agreement** and define:

- What rights are granted
- Duration and territory
- Usage limits
- Payment terms

## Final Thoughts

Your art is your asset. Your ideas have value. But unless you protect them, others can exploit them—intentionally or not.

Learn your rights. Use the tools. Respect others' work—and expect the same.

Your voice is unique. Guard it fiercely. And when needed—defend it legally.

This is how you turn talent into legacy.

# Chapter 35: Hiring the Right Team – CPAs, Financial Advisors, Agents, and Attorneys

You don't have to do everything alone. In fact, building a smart, trustworthy team is one of the best financial decisions you can make as an artist. The right professionals can help you keep more of what you earn, grow your wealth, avoid legal pitfalls, and protect your rights.

This chapter walks you through the key players to consider for your team, what they do, how they get paid, and how to find ones you can trust.

## Why Building a Financial Team Matters

- You're not just creating art—you're running a business
- You have income, taxes, contracts, and long-term goals to manage
- Experts help you avoid expensive mistakes and save time

## Key Players on Your Financial Support Team

### *1. CPA (Certified Public Accountant)*

**What They Do:**

- Help you prepare and file taxes

- Advise on deductions and tax strategies
- Assist with business entity formation

**Why You Need One:**

- Artists often have complex income (freelance, licensing, sales)
- A good CPA can help you save thousands by properly categorizing expenses

**How They're Paid:**

- Hourly or flat fee (especially for tax prep)

**Tips:**

- Look for a CPA with experience working with creatives or freelancers

### *2. Financial Advisor*

**What They Do:**

- Help you set goals and build a financial plan
- Assist with investing, retirement, insurance, and budgeting
- Guide big-picture decision-making over time

**Why You Need One:**

- To grow your money and manage it wisely
- To avoid common investment mistakes

**How They're Paid:**

- Fee-only (hourly or flat rate)

- Percentage of assets under management (AUM)
- Commission-based (less recommended—may involve conflicts of interest)

**Tips:**

- Look for a fiduciary who puts your interests first
- Ask for credentials (e.g., CFP® designation)

## *3. Agent or Representative*

**What They Do:**

- Negotiate contracts, book gigs, and find opportunities
- Take a percentage of what you earn from those deals

**Why You Need One:**

- When your time is better spent creating than pitching or negotiating
- When opportunities are coming in faster than you can manage

**How They're Paid:**

- Typically 10–20% of earnings from booked work

**Tips:**

- Choose someone who understands your field and respects your vision
- Get terms in writing—always

### *4. Attorney (Especially an Entertainment or IP Lawyer)*

**What They Do:**

- Draft and review contracts
- Help you protect your intellectual property
- Advise on business formation, disputes, and licensing

**Why You Need One:**

- To avoid signing bad deals or giving away your rights
- To protect your brand, your work, and your future income

**How They're Paid:**

- Hourly rates, flat fees, or retainer agreements

**Tips:**

- Seek someone who works with creatives or small businesses
- Don't wait until you're in trouble to find a good attorney

## How to Find the Right Professionals

- Ask fellow artists who they use and trust
- Use directories like:
- CFP Board (financial advisors)
- AICPA (CPAs)
- Volunteer Lawyers for the Arts
- Interview multiple people
- Trust your instincts and watch for red flags (pushy, unclear, unresponsive)

## Final Thoughts

You don't need to become an expert in taxes, investing, or contracts.

But you do need a team who is.

Start building relationships with the professionals who can help you protect your career, grow your money, and stay focused on what you do best: creating.

When your art is your business, treat it like one—and surround yourself with the right people to help it thrive.

# Chapter 36: Estate Planning for Creatives – Wills, Trusts, and Protecting Your Work

As a creative, your legacy isn't just money—it's your art, your voice, your intellectual property, and the story you've built through your work. Estate planning ensures that your work and assets are handled the way *you* want—not just what the courts decide.

This chapter walks you through how to prepare, protect, and pass on your creative life's work with intention.

## Why Estate Planning Matters for Artists

- You may have copyrights, royalties, or licensing agreements to manage
- You might want to control how your work is used or remembered after your death
- Even if you don't have a lot of money, you have creative assets worth protecting

## Key Components of an Estate Plan

### *1. Will*

**What it does:**

- Specifies who inherits your belongings

- Names guardians for dependents (if any)
- Appoints an executor to carry out your wishes

**Artist-specific tip:** Include your creative assets in the will (physical and digital artwork, copyrights, royalties, etc.)

### *2. Trust*

**What it does:**

- Holds and manages assets for your beneficiaries
- Can distribute assets over time, protect privacy, and avoid probate

**Why use one:**

- Helpful if you have intellectual property or expect ongoing income from your art

### *3. Power of Attorney*

- Appoints someone to manage your finances if you become incapacitated

### *4. Healthcare Directive / Living Will*

- Names someone to make medical decisions for you
- States your preferences for end-of-life care

## Protecting Your Creative Work

### *Document Ownership and Rights*

- Keep records of what you created and when
- Include a list of copyright registrations and trademarks

### *Decide What Happens to Your Work*

- Do you want someone to manage your website, social media, and online store?
- Should your art continue to be sold, archived, or retired?
- Can family members license your work? If so, how?

### *Assign a Literary/Artistic Executor*

- Choose someone who understands your work and can manage your artistic estate
- Give them authority in your will or trust to act on your behalf

## Steps to Get Started

1. **List your creative and financial assets**
2. **Decide who should receive what**
3. **Talk with a lawyer familiar with artists' estates**
4. **Create or update your will and/or trust**
5. **Name backups in case someone is unavailable**
6. **Store your documents safely and tell someone where they are**

## Tools and Resources

- Volunteer Lawyers for the Arts (VLA)
- California Lawyers for the Arts (useful nationally)
- NOLO.com for DIY will/trust resources
- Estate planning attorneys with creative clients

## Final Thoughts

Estate planning isn't just about death—it's about dignity, control, and clarity.

As a creative, your legacy is rich and meaningful. Don't leave it to chance.

Make the plan. Protect the work. Pass it on—your way.

That's how you keep your story alive, even when you're not here to tell it.

# Chapter 37: Avoiding Scams, Bad Deals, and Predatory Practices

Artists are often passionate, trusting, and eager for opportunity—which can make them prime targets for scams, shady deals, and predatory contracts. Whether it's a fake gallery, a misleading contest, or an exploitative "exposure" opportunity, knowing the red flags can save your money, your rights, and your reputation.

This chapter is about protecting your creative career from the people and deals that don't have your best interests at heart.

## Why Artists Are Often Targeted

- Many creatives work independently with limited business experience
- There's a deep desire for visibility and recognition
- The promise of money or exposure can cloud judgment

That's why understanding how scams work—and how to spot them—is a form of self-defense.

## Common Artist Scams and Traps

### *1. Pay-to-Play Galleries or Exhibits*

- You're asked to pay high fees upfront to "show your work"
- These shows are often poorly curated and provide little real value

**What to do:**

- Research the gallery's reputation
- Ask for past artist testimonials
- Compare to established galleries that pay *you* for work

### *2. Vanity Contests or Awards*

- You win—but you're asked to pay a fee to be "featured" in a book or show
- There's often no real judging or value

**What to do:**

- Look for contests with transparent juries and no entry or winner's fee
- Prioritize competitions backed by reputable institutions

### *3. "We'll Use Your Art for Exposure"*

- You're asked to design, perform, or create for free with the promise of exposure or future opportunities

**What to do:**

- Exposure doesn't pay the bills—be cautious
- If you choose to donate work, do so strategically (for charities or causes you truly support)

### *4. Licensing or Royalties With No Upfront Pay*

- You're offered vague "royalty shares" in exchange for use of your work—but no contract or details

**What to do:**

- Insist on written agreements
- Know what rights you're giving away and how payment works

### *5. Fake Buyers or Overpayment Scams*

- Someone "buys" your art and sends a check for too much, asking you to refund the extra
- The original check later bounces

**What to do:**

- Never refund money before a payment fully clears
- Avoid shipping artwork before receiving confirmed payment

## How to Spot Red Flags

- Vague communication or evasive answers
- High-pressure tactics ("This opportunity will disappear in 24 hours!")
- Unusually high fees or upfront payments
- No contract, or one that's heavily one-sided
- Promises that sound too good to be true

## How to Protect Yourself

### *Always Research First*

- Google the organization, person, or offer
- Look up artist forums or Facebook groups for past experiences

### *Ask Questions*

- Who is funding the project?
- How will your work be used?
- What rights are you giving up?

### *Get It in Writing*

- Always request a clear, written contract or agreement
- Don't rely on verbal promises or vague emails

### *Don't Be Afraid to Walk Away*

- If something feels off, trust your gut
- No opportunity is worth giving up your rights or financial security

## Tools and Resources

- Volunteer Lawyers for the Arts
- Artists' Union or Guild organizations
- Reddit: r/ArtBusiness, r/Freelance
- Facebook groups for freelance artists

## Final Thoughts

You've worked too hard to let someone take advantage of you.

A smart artist isn't just creative—they're cautious, curious, and careful.

Stay skeptical. Ask questions. Do your research. And remember: the real deal respects your time, your rights, and your worth.

You deserve more than empty promises. You deserve contracts, compensation, and career respect.

Be informed. Be assertive. And never be afraid to say "no" to a bad deal.

# Chapter 38: Exit Strategies – Selling a Business, Licensing Your Work Long-Term, or Retiring from Performing

Every artist has a journey—and at some point, that journey shifts. Maybe you're ready to move on from the business side of your art. Maybe your energy is shifting toward mentorship or other pursuits. Maybe you're simply planning for the day when you want to step back.

Exit strategies don't mean giving up. They mean planning ahead so your creative work and income can keep working—even when you're not.

This chapter outlines how to leave on your terms, whether by selling your business, licensing your art for long-term use, or stepping away from live performance.

## Why You Need an Exit Strategy

- Your body, schedule, or interests may change
- You deserve peace of mind and financial security
- Proper planning allows your work to outlive your day-to-day involvement

## Option 1: Selling a Creative Business

If you've built a brand, studio, platform, or product that generates revenue, you may be able to sell it.

### *What You Can Sell:*

- Physical assets (equipment, tools, inventory)
- Brand name, logo, or website
- Email list, customer base, and goodwill
- Intellectual property or content libraries

### *Steps to Sell:*

1. **Get your business financials in order**
2. **Document systems and processes**
3. **Consult with a business broker or attorney**
4. **Value your business based on income and assets**
5. **Find a buyer through your network or platforms like BizBuySell**

### *Pros:*

- Lump sum or payment plan
- Freedom to move on

### *Cons:*

- Letting go of control
- Possible emotional detachment

## Option 2: Licensing Your Work for Long-Term Use

Instead of selling, you can keep ownership and license your work to others.

### *Examples:*

- Licensing art for merchandise, books, or digital use
- Music licensing for film, TV, or commercials
- Creating recurring content for brands

### *How to Do It:*

- Register your intellectual property (copyright, trademark)
- Create a licensing agreement (define terms, usage, time frame, payment)
- Partner with a licensing agency or do it independently

### *Pros:*

- Recurring passive income
- Retain ownership

### *Cons:*

- Requires ongoing management or legal oversight

## Option 3: Retiring from Performing or Touring

If you're a performer—musician, dancer, actor—retirement might look like:

- Slowing down bookings
- Creating recorded versions of your work
- Shifting into teaching or coaching
- Writing a memoir or course

*Planning Your Exit:*

- Save and invest regularly to fund retirement
- Build online products to replace live income
- Document your legacy for future licensing

## Tools to Support Your Exit

- Financial advisor for retirement planning
- Attorney for licensing or business sale contracts
- Accountant for tax strategy
- Digital archive of your work for future monetization

## Final Thoughts

Your creative path doesn't end with a curtain call. It evolves.

Whether you're planning your exit now or years from now, the key is to be proactive.

Plan the handoff. Monetize the legacy. And remember: stepping back doesn't mean stopping.

It means building a bridge—from what you've created to what will continue.

Exit gracefully. Exit intentionally. Exit with your art still earning for you.

# Part VI: Life, Legacy, and Long-Term Planning

**Planning for the Art of a Lifetime—and Beyond**

This final section is about thinking beyond the next gig or grant. It's about building a life—not just a career—that aligns with your values, sustains your creativity, and leaves a lasting impact. Whether you're designing a graceful exit from the stage, preparing to pass down your work, or finally taking control of your financial future, this part helps you zoom out and think big.

Inside, you'll learn how to:

- Protect your art and income through estate planning
- Hire the right advisors and professionals to support your vision
- Avoid scams and predatory practices that target creatives
- Exit your creative career on your own terms—through selling, licensing, or retiring
- Turn your work into a legacy that supports future generations

Part VI is about future-proofing your journey—so your work, your values, and your wealth keep working, even when you decide to rest.

# Chapter 39: Giving Back – Supporting Your Community and Charitable Giving

As artists, we don't just create for ourselves—we create for connection, culture, and community. And as you grow in your financial literacy and success, giving back can become a meaningful part of your journey.

Whether it's donating time, money, art, or mentorship, this chapter explores how to give in ways that are sustainable, impactful, and aligned with your values.

## Why Giving Back Matters

- Strengthens the communities that inspired you
- Shares access to resources you didn't always have
- Creates opportunities for the next generation of creatives
- Enhances personal purpose and fulfillment

## Ways to Give Back as an Artist

### *1. Donate Your Time*

- Teach workshops or mentor younger artists
- Volunteer at local arts nonprofits, schools, or community centers
- Join boards or advisory panels for creative organizations

### *2. Donate Art or Creative Services*

- Contribute work to auctions or fundraisers
- Offer design, music, or photography services for community events or causes
- Collaborate with nonprofits on awareness campaigns

### *3. Financial Contributions*

- Give to causes you care about (arts education, social justice, mental health, etc.)
- Set up recurring donations that fit your budget
- Include charitable giving in your estate plan

### *4. Create a Giving Fund*

- Open a donor-advised fund (DAF) if you want to structure your giving more formally
- Use it to contribute to multiple nonprofits while receiving immediate tax benefits

## Choosing Where to Give

- What causes align with your personal story or values?
- Is the organization transparent and effective?
- Does it support your local community or a mission you believe in?

**Tip:** Research nonprofits on platforms like GuideStar or Charity Navigator

## Making It Sustainable

You don't have to give huge amounts of time or money. Consistency matters more than size.

- Set a monthly giving budget
- Block off volunteer days on your calendar
- Collaborate with other artists to amplify your impact

## Giving as a Legacy Strategy

- Include nonprofits in your will or trust
- Donate rights to your work to a museum, archive, or institution
- Create an artist scholarship or residency in your name

## Final Thoughts

You've spent your life expressing yourself, creating meaning, and navigating the ups and downs of a creative path. Now you have the opportunity to use your resources—however big or small—to uplift others.

Giving back isn't just generous. It's strategic. It's legacy. It's how we build a creative economy that works for everyone.

Give what you can. Give how you can. And give in a way that keeps your values—and your voice—alive.

# Chapter 40: Financial Literacy for Artist Parents – Teaching Your Kids About Money and Creativity

Being an artist and a parent is a balancing act of creativity, responsibility, and values. You're not just shaping your art—you're shaping a household, a mindset, and a future generation. This chapter is about passing on the lessons you've learned as a creative and financially aware adult so your kids can grow up with confidence around both money and imagination.

## Why It Matters

- Many of us didn't grow up learning about money—or how to turn passion into income
- Kids watch what you do more than what you say
- By modeling healthy money habits and creativity, you give your children tools for both freedom and fulfillment

## Start with Conversations, Not Lectures

- Talk openly about how you earn money as an artist
- Let them see you budgeting, saving, and planning
- Normalize money conversations as part of everyday life

Example: "I sold two paintings this month, and I'm saving some of that to pay for your art camp."

## Key Concepts to Teach Kids (By Age)

*Ages 4–7:*

- What money is and how it's earned
- Saving in a piggy bank or clear jar
- That creative work has value (e.g., paying them a few dollars for making cards)

*Ages 8–12:*

- Allowance tied to simple chores or creative tasks
- Setting short-term savings goals
- Introduction to spending, saving, and giving jars

*Ages 13–17:*

- Budgeting basics (food, gas, fun)
- Starting a bank account
- Making money from hobbies (selling art, commissions, teaching younger kids)

## Encouraging Creativity as a Financial Skill

- Show how you turn ideas into income
- Support their creative ventures (Etsy shops, TikTok tutorials, beat making, crafts)
- Teach the balance between creative expression and business structure

## Tools and Activities

- Family budget board (visual tracker of goals and spending)
- "Business of Art" conversations over dinner
- Creative entrepreneurship projects (e.g., host an art show at home)
- Books, games, and apps that teach money (e.g., Greenlight, FamZoo, Money Quest)

## Talking About Mistakes

- Share financial missteps you've made (age-appropriate)
- Model how you recover, learn, and move forward
- Teach them that mistakes aren't failures—they're part of growth

## Long-Term Lessons for Your Kids

- Money is a tool, not a goal
- Passion and practicality can coexist
- Their creativity has value—and so does planning
- They are capable of building a life that reflects their art *and* their financial goals

## Final Thoughts

Being an artist parent is a chance to raise not just good kids, but creative, confident, financially literate humans.

Start early. Keep it simple. Be consistent.

Give them the paintbrush—and the plan. Let them build a future that's bold, imaginative, and financially free.

That's the legacy of an artist parent who gets it—and passes it on.

# Chapter 41: Burnout, Breaks, and Budgeting for Time Off

In the world of art, hustle culture is real. The pressure to produce, perform, and stay relevant can leave you mentally, emotionally, and physically drained. But here's the truth: taking breaks isn't a luxury—it's a necessity. And just like you budget for rent or supplies, you can and should budget for rest.

This chapter explores how to prevent burnout, plan intentional breaks, and create a financial system that supports your well-being as much as your work.

## What Is Burnout?

Burnout is chronic physical and emotional exhaustion caused by prolonged stress or overwork. For artists, it can feel like:

- Loss of motivation or inspiration
- Resentment toward your craft or clients
- Constant fatigue or illness
- Creative block that won't lift

Burnout doesn't just affect your art—it affects your income, relationships, and mental health.

## Why Budgeting for Time Off Matters

- Prevents long-term mental and physical health issues
- Gives space for reflection, experimentation, and creative reset
- Supports sustainable income and inspiration over time

Taking a break doesn't mean you're lazy. It means you understand your energy is a resource to protect.

## How to Recognize When You Need a Break

- You dread opening your laptop or studio door
- You've stopped enjoying work you used to love
- You're working more but earning less
- Your personal relationships are suffering

If you're nodding yes—it's time to plan a pause.

## Types of Breaks to Consider

### *Micro-Breaks (Daily/Weekly)*

- 10–20 minute breaks throughout your workday
- One day per week completely unplugged

### *Mini Sabbaticals (1–2 weeks)*

- Planned time off to reset, retreat, or travel
- Focus on rest or non-revenue creativity

### *Full Hiatus (1+ month)*

- Stepping back from projects, commissions, or gigs
- Often aligned with a life shift or deep burnout

## Budgeting for Time Off

### *Step 1: Know Your Monthly Burn Rate*

- Calculate basic expenses: rent, food, utilities, transportation, insurance

### *Step 2: Set a Break Budget*

- Decide how much time you want off
- Multiply your monthly expenses by that time frame
- Add a cushion (10–20%) for emergencies or extras

### *Step 3: Create a Time-Off Fund*

- Open a separate savings account just for breaks
- Auto-transfer a portion of each payment to that account

Example: Save $200/month = $2,400 in a year (enough for 1 month off)

## Creative Ways to Earn While Resting

- Passive income from licensing, digital products, or online courses
- Schedule posts and email marketing in advance
- Batch client work ahead of your break

## Communication and Boundaries

- Let clients or collaborators know you'll be unavailable (with notice)
- Use auto-responders or delegation tools
- Turn off notifications and resist the urge to "just check in"

## What to Do During Your Break

- Rest without guilt
- Travel, journal, read, or do non-art hobbies
- Reflect on your goals, habits, and direction

## Final Thoughts

Breaks aren't setbacks. They're strategy.

You don't have to earn burnout to deserve rest. And you don't have to wait until you're falling apart to step away.

Start small. Save consistently. Schedule breaks the same way you schedule gigs.

Because your creativity isn't just what you produce. It's what you protect.

And when you invest in rest, your art—and your life—gets better.

# Chapter 42: Designing a Life of Creative and Financial Freedom

Creative freedom and financial freedom aren't opposites—they're partners. One fuels your spirit, the other supports your stability. When you combine the two, you unlock the ability to live life on your terms, making work that matters to you without compromising your well-being or your wallet.

This chapter is about intentional living—designing a career and lifestyle that reflect your values, passions, and long-term goals.

## What Does Creative and Financial Freedom Look Like?

- Making the art you want, not just what pays the bills
- Choosing clients and projects based on fit, not desperation
- Living in alignment with your values and vision
- Having money to rest, take risks, invest, and give back
- Knowing your income is stable and sustainable

## Step 1: Define What Freedom Means to You

Your version of freedom might include:

- Working 4 days a week
- Living somewhere inspiring

- Touring part-time and teaching part-time
- Building passive income from your work

Freedom isn't about a number—it's about *choice.*

Write it out. Visualize your ideal day, week, or year. Then reverse-engineer your plan.

## Step 2: Build a Vision-Aligned Budget

Create a spending plan that reflects what you actually want.

- Cut costs that don't support your creative or life goals
- Prioritize savings, investing, and time-off funds
- Fund your dream studio, residency, or sabbatical

Your budget is your blueprint. Make sure it builds the life you want.

## Step 3: Diversify Your Income

The more income streams you have, the more options you create.

- Active: client work, sales, gigs
- Semi-passive: courses, prints, digital downloads
- Passive: royalties, licensing, investments

This isn't about overworking—it's about building systems that work for you.

## Step 4: Schedule Rest, Joy, and Space

Time is just as important as money.

- Block off creative recharge time

- Set non-negotiable days off
- Take trips, artist dates, or solo retreats

Protecting your energy is part of protecting your freedom.

## Step 5: Invest in Yourself and Your Future

Put your money where your values are.

- Fund your education, equipment, or creative development
- Save for long-term goals: retirement, home studio, legacy
- Work with financial advisors who respect your creative life

## Step 6: Revisit and Redesign Regularly

Life shifts. So should your plan.

- Check in with your goals every 3–6 months
- Adjust for new projects, seasons, or priorities
- Celebrate progress—even the small wins

## Final Thoughts

You are the architect of your creative life.

You don't need to follow someone else's path to success. You get to design your own—one that's rich in meaning *and* stability.

Design with intention. Budget with purpose. Work with freedom.

Because the best life is one where your art flows—and your finances follow.

# Chapter 43: What Is the Market, the Economy, and Everything Else You See on TV?

**Understanding the Market: A Creative's Guide to Investing**

You've probably heard headlines like:

"The market is crashing!"

"The S&P 500 is soaring!"

"The Fed raised interest rates again!"

"Inflation is out of control!"

It's enough to make anyone want to tune out and just go back to painting, writing, recording, or creating.

But here's the truth: once you understand how the market works, it stops being intimidating—and starts becoming one of your most powerful creative tools. Think of the financial world like a big, unpredictable art show. There are themes, movements, critics, fans, trends—and tons of emotion.

Let's break it down with examples that actually make sense for your world.

**What Is the Stock Market?**

The stock market is where people buy and sell pieces of companies. These pieces are called *shares*. When you buy stock in a company like Adobe or Apple, you own a tiny part of it.

Artist analogy: Think of it like getting royalties every time your art sells. The better the company does, the more valuable your "share" becomes.

**Why Do Prices Go Up and Down?**

It's all about supply and demand. If more people want a stock, the price rises. If more people want to sell it, the price falls. News, politics, earnings reports—even tweets—can influence this.

Artist analogy: It's like buzz at an art fair. If people love your latest series, your work sells out and prices rise. If reviews are bad or no one shows up, sales dip.

**Stock Market vs. The Economy—Aren't They the Same?**

Nope. The market is based on investor emotions and predictions. The economy is what's actually happening—jobs, spending, production.

Artist analogy: The market is your social media feed. The economy is your actual bank account.

**Is the Market Risky? Can I Lose Money?**

Yes, there's risk. If you invest in just one company and it tanks, you could lose a lot. But if you invest across many companies (through an index fund or ETF), you spread out that risk.

Artist analogy: It's like only selling one piece of art versus having a full collection across galleries and platforms.

**What's the Smart Way to Start Investing?**

- Use index funds or ETFs (they include hundreds of companies)
- Open a Roth IRA or brokerage account
- Stay consistent
- Think long-term

Artist analogy: It's like building a portfolio. You don't need one breakout piece—you need consistent, solid work that builds value over time.

**When Should I Start?**

Now. Always now. The earlier you start, the longer your money has to grow.

Artist analogy: The earlier you start promoting your work or building an audience, the bigger your following becomes. Same with investing.

**What Is the S&P 500?**

It's a list of the 500 largest U.S. companies. It's like the "Top 500 Artists" chart for business. If those companies are thriving, the market is likely doing well.

**Bull vs. Bear Markets**

- *Bull Market:* Prices rising, confidence high
- *Bear Market:* Prices dropping, people are nervous

Artist analogy: A bull market is like your art going viral. A bear market is when sales are slow and no one's buying.

**Should I Sell When Prices Drop?**

No. Selling during a drop locks in your losses. Stay calm and ride it out.

Artist analogy: If one painting doesn't sell right away, you don't quit art altogether. You keep showing up.

**How Much Do I Need to Start?**

You can begin with $50 or $100. Platforms let you buy fractional shares.

Artist analogy: You don't need a studio in Manhattan to start. You just need a corner and a brush.

**Can I Make Fast Money in the Market?**

Technically yes—but that's gambling, not investing.

Artist analogy: Anyone can go viral once. True success comes from creating consistently, building trust, and showing up year after year.

**What's an ETF?**

An ETF (Exchange-Traded Fund) bundles many investments into one. It's like creating a zine of your best work instead of trying to sell each page individually.

**Is Investing Only for the Wealthy?**

Not at all. Investing is how you become wealthy. Start small, stay consistent.

**Stocks vs. Bonds?**

- *Stock:* You own part of a company
- *Bond:* You're lending money to a company or government

Artist analogy: Stock is like owning the gallery. Bond is like loaning money to help run it.

**What's Diversification?**

It's spreading your money across many types of investments. Don't put everything in one place.

Artist analogy: You don't show the same painting at every exhibition. You spread your work across different shows, audiences, and formats.

**Why "Buy Low, Sell High"?**

That's how you profit. But most people do the opposite—they buy high from hype and sell low in fear.

**How Do I Know What to Invest In?**

Start with index funds and ETFs. Keep fees low. Reinvest dividends. Think long-term.

**What Happens in a Recession?**

The economy slows, people spend less, markets dip. It's like winter for creatives—quiet, reflective, maybe slow on income—but it passes.

**Do I Need a Financial Advisor?**

Not at first. You can start solo. But if your income grows or things get complicated, it helps to have a pro.

**#1 Rule of Investing?**

Start early. Be consistent. Don't panic.

**What's a Dividend?**

Some companies pay a portion of their profits to shareholders. That's a dividend.

Artist analogy: It's like getting royalties from prints you sold last year.

**How Often Should I Check My Investments?**

Not often. Once a month is plenty.

**What's a Stock Split?**

When a company's stock becomes expensive, they split it into more affordable pieces. You still own the same value.

**What's a Market Correction?**

A normal 10% dip. Not a crash. Just a breather.

**Should I Invest if Prices Are Dropping?**

Yes. Things are on sale.

**Can I Lose It All?**

Only if you bet everything on one risky investment. Diversify, and you're likely to bounce back—even in downturns.

**Mutual Funds vs. ETFs?**

Both hold many investments. ETFs usually have lower fees and more flexibility.

**What Are Interest Rates?**

It's the cost of borrowing money. When rates go up, everything slows down—including the market.

**What's Dollar-Cost Averaging?**

Invest the same amount regularly, no matter what the market is doing. Over time, it averages out.

Artist analogy: Like working on your art every week. Sometimes you're inspired, sometimes not—but the work adds up.

**Final Thoughts: Invest Like an Artist**

The market is just another creative ecosystem—messy, unpredictable, emotional. But with time and discipline, you can learn to play the long game.

- Diversify like you curate your portfolio
- Stay consistent like you practice your craft
- Don't panic like it's your first show

Investing isn't about being lucky. It's about being prepared.

The market is one more canvas. Paint your future with intention.

# Chapter 44: You Love Them. But You Can't Save Them All

*How to Set Boundaries When the Money Starts Flowing*

Let's talk about one of the hardest parts of coming into money as an artist—especially when you're the first in your family or friend group to do so.

You finally booked a big commission.

You sold out a gallery show.

Your music blew up on streaming.

You just signed a licensing deal that changed everything.

And now—everyone needs help.

Helping your mom who supported your art since you were sketching on the kitchen table? You want to.

Helping your dad fix the car so he can get to work? Of course.

Helping a cousin or friend who's struggling? They were there before anyone cared about your art.

You want to be generous. You want to be loyal. You want to give back.

But here's the truth:

**If you're not careful, you'll drain everything you've worked for trying to save everyone else.**

This chapter is about helping with boundaries—not burnout. About being generous without being broke. About creating a future where you don't have to say, "I used to make money from my art..."

## *Start Here: You're Not the Family's Retirement Plan*

If you're the first in your family to "make it," people may assume your money is *our* money. They'll ask. Some won't ask—they'll just expect.

But even if you do want to help: You are not the emergency fund.

You are not the bank.

You are not a never-ending checkbook.

If you decide to give, it has to be with intention.

## *Option 1: The Monthly Support Budget*

Let's say you want to help your mom with groceries or rent.

You set a monthly "family support" budget:

**$500 total per month. No more.**

Break it up like this:

- $200 to her landlord or mortgage company (paid directly)
- $200 for groceries or utilities
- $100 on a prepaid debit card for miscellaneous

Once you hit $500 for the month, that's it.

If someone else calls?

You say:

> *"I've already reached my family support budget for the month. Let's talk next month."*

That's not cold—it's clarity. That's not selfish—it's structure.

### *Option 2: The One-Time Gift*

Don't want the monthly pressure? Give a lump sum and be done.

Let's say you just got a $15,000 advance from a record label or sold a piece for $10,000. You decide you can afford to give $1,500 to help your parents with overdue bills.

You say:

> *"This is a one-time gift. I wanted to do something meaningful, and I'm glad I can. But I won't be able to give more right now."*

Then you stick to it. No "just one more."

No guilt. No negotiation.

It's a gift, not a subscription.

### *What If It's More Than One Person?*

Let's say you've got three people asking for help: your mom, your brother, and your best friend.

Set a **total** monthly or annual budget, and divide it *if you choose.*

Example:

- Total yearly support = $6,000
- That's $500/month max
- Mom: $300
- Brother: $100
- Best friend: $100

You don't adjust because someone cries harder.

You don't feel guilty when you say no.

This is **your** financial plan.

They fit inside it—or they don't.

### *Say It Early, Say It Clearly*

If you don't clearly say how much you're willing to give, people will assume it's unlimited. And assumptions lead to tension, drama, and burnout.

Have the hard talk. Set the boundary.

You say:

> *"I'm proud to be able to help. But I've created a support budget. Once I hit that number, I can't go over it. This is how I'm protecting my future."*

And when they say, "But just this once..."

You say no. Firmly. Lovingly. With peace.

### *Signs You're Enabling, Not Helping*

If any of these start happening, it's time to rethink your approach:

- They stop trying to help themselves
- They act like your help is guaranteed
- They guilt you when you say no
- You keep paying for the same crisis
- You feel resentment building

Instead of giving cash:

- Pay the bill directly
- Offer help finding work
- Share financial literacy tools
- Make the help *temporary*

Because if someone needs $200 every month to stay afloat, what they need isn't money—they need a plan.

## *If They Get Mad, Let Them*

Setting boundaries will make some people upset—especially if they're used to "yes."

They may say:

> *"You changed."*
> *"You forgot where you came from."*
> *"You think you're better now."*

Let them.

You're not here to earn everyone's approval.

You're here to build something real, something sustainable.

In five or ten years, when you're still creating, still financially strong, still in control—they'll understand.

## *Final Thoughts: Give With Boundaries, Not Guilt*

You're not wrong for saying no.

You're not cold for setting limits.

You're not selfish for choosing your future.

If you decide to help: Do it with a plan.

Do it without shame.

Do it in a way that protects your peace, your art, and your financial freedom.

The most powerful gift you can give isn't a handout—it's an example.

Of financial strength.

Of emotional discipline.

Of what's possible when an artist leads with both creativity and clarity.

That's love. That's wisdom.

That's legacy.

# Chapter 45: Don't Just Get Paid. Build Something With It.

You just got paid.

Maybe it was your first big art commission.

Maybe a licensing deal came through.

Maybe a festival check or a $10,000 mural job finally hit your account.

Whatever the number—$1,000 or $100,000—the feeling is the same: "I made this with my talent."

So now what?

Do you splurge? Cop the designer bag? Upgrade the gear? Fly somewhere sunny to decompress?

Sure, celebrate a little. But the real move?

**Build something with it.**

Because when you're an artist, income can come fast... and disappear just as quickly.

This chapter is about what comes *next*. How to take the money you earned and grow it. How to invest. How to choose the right account. How to make it count—so it's not just a good day, it's the start of a good life.

## *Step 1: What Does Investing Really Mean?*

Investing is putting your money to work *for you*.

Instead of leaving it to sit (or letting it vanish into meals, merch, and impulse buys), you put it in vehicles that grow—like stocks, index funds,

ETFs, or bonds.

If you do it right—and do it early—your money will multiply without needing you to constantly grind for it.

### *Step 2: Know Your Goals and Your Time Frame*

Before you invest, ask yourself:

- Will I need this money soon (for rent, tuition, or a new camera)?
- Can I afford to leave it alone for 3–5+ years?
- Am I trying to build long-term wealth or flip it fast?

If you can leave it alone for at least 5 years, investing is a smart move. But if you'll need it in 3 months, keep that part in cash.

### *Step 3: Pick Your Investment Account*

Different accounts have different rules—and benefits. Here's the artist-friendly rundown:

**Roth IRA**

- Contribute with after-tax money
- Grows tax-free
- Withdraw in retirement = *no taxes at all*
- Limit: $6,500 per year (as of 2025)
- Must have earned income

**Why it's great for artists:**

You're likely in a lower tax bracket now. Pay taxes now, and your money grows completely tax-free for decades.

# Chapter 46: Broke After the Spotlight – Famous Artists Who Lost It All

You can have the talent, the vision, and the recognition—and still lose everything.

This chapter isn't about shame. It's about learning. Because the truth is, many brilliant artists fell into financial ruin not because they weren't talented—but because they didn't have a plan. Let's look at some of the most well-known painters, actors, photographers, and filmmakers who saw millions come and go.

## *1. Annie Leibovitz – Photographer*

**Known For:** Iconic celebrity portraits for *Vanity Fair, Rolling Stone,* and *Vogue*

**What Happened:** At the height of her success, Leibovitz took out high-interest loans against her work and properties to fund an expensive lifestyle. In 2009, she was $24 million in debt and nearly lost the rights to her entire portfolio.

**Lesson:** Even with a world-class portfolio, cash flow and debt management matter. Don't borrow more than you can manage—especially against your intellectual property.

### *2. Kim Basinger – Actor*

**Known For:** *Batman, L.A. Confidential,* Oscar-winning career

**What Happened:** In the early '90s, Basinger bought an entire town in Georgia for $20 million, hoping to turn it into a tourist attraction. The project failed. Then she backed out of a movie contract (*Boxing Helena*), was sued for breach, and filed for bankruptcy.

**Lesson:** Don't overextend on speculative ventures. Understand contract obligations, and always have legal and financial counsel before big decisions.

### *3. Basquiat – Painter*

**Known For:** Neo-expressionist work in the 1980s, collaborations with Warhol

**What Happened:** While Basquiat earned fame and significant income during his short career, he struggled with money management, substance abuse, and navigating fame. At the time of his death, many financial details of his estate were left unclear and unplanned.

**Lesson:** Artistic genius doesn't replace the need for a financial strategy and an estate plan.

### *4. Wesley Snipes – Actor*

**Known For:** *Blade* series, *White Men Can't Jump, New Jack City*

**What Happened:** Snipes failed to pay taxes for years, believing he didn't legally have to. He was convicted of tax evasion and served prison time.

**Lesson:** Even if you don't understand the tax code, the IRS still expects you to comply. Hire a CPA. Always.

### *5. Toni Braxton – Performer / Theater Actress*

**Known For:** Grammy-winning music and Broadway performances

**What Happened:** Braxton filed bankruptcy twice. First in 1998 after sales didn't match her contract expectations, and again in 2010 due to health issues that forced her to cancel performances.

**Lesson:** Know what your contract *actually* says. Protect your income with insurance, and build an emergency fund to support downtime.

### *6. Francis Bacon – Painter*

**Known For:** Bold, unsettling portraits and figure studies

**What Happened:** Though his works eventually sold for millions, Bacon often lived modestly and gave away paintings without concern for their future value. He died without a detailed estate plan, and disputes over his work continue today.

**Lesson:** Estate planning matters. Your art is your legacy—protect it legally and financially while you're alive.

### *7. Nicolas Cage – Actor*

**Known For:** *Leaving Las Vegas, National Treasure, Face/Off*

**What Happened:** Cage earned over $150 million, but blew it on real estate, exotic cars, castles, rare artifacts (like dinosaur skulls), and eccentric purchases. He owed millions in back taxes.

**Lesson:** It's not about how much you earn—it's about how you manage it. Budget. Delegate. And don't let lifestyle outpace reality.

### *8. David LaChapelle – Photographer / Director*

**Known For:** Hyper-stylized celebrity photos and music videos

**What Happened:** LaChapelle walked away from commercial photography due to burnout and financial complications, choosing to retreat to

Hawaii. His income dropped significantly before reinventing his work.

**Lesson:** Burnout is real—and so is inconsistent income. Always plan for breaks, pivots, and mental health care.

### *9. Michael Vick – Athlete turned Filmmaker & Advocate*

**Known For:** NFL star, later produced documentaries and films

**What Happened:** Declared bankruptcy in 2008 after legal troubles and overspending. His comeback included storytelling through documentaries—but rebuilding took years.

**Lesson:** Reinvention is possible—but it's easier if you never lose control of your money to begin with.

### *10. Judy Garland – Actor / Singer*

**Known For:** *The Wizard of Oz*, legendary stage performances

**What Happened:** Despite global fame, Garland struggled with finances due to addiction, mismanagement, and poor contracts. She owed massive amounts in back taxes and died with little to her name.

**Lesson:** Watch your team. Understand your income. And protect your brand while you still have the power to do so.

## Final Thoughts: Don't Let Fame Fool You

Fame is loud. Money is quiet. And when the spotlight fades, it's your financial decisions—not your fan base—that will determine whether you survive or thrive.

Whether you're painting, producing, performing, or photographing:

- Know your contracts
- Track your money
- Work with a team of trusted professionals
- Stay humble about your income

- Protect your mental health
- Build wealth that outlasts applause

Talent opens doors. But financial literacy keeps them open.

Let their losses become your lessons. So you can focus on what you do best—creating.

# Chapter 47: What's a Portfolio? Build Your Plan, Diversify Your Lineup

**Every Artist Needs a Game Plan**

Think of your financial future like your biggest creative project—a gallery opening, a record launch, a film premiere. You wouldn't show up without a concept, structure, and intention. You'd plan every detail. The same applies to your money.

That's what a portfolio is. It's your financial body of work—a collection of different investments, each with a specific role. When you build a smart portfolio, you're not just chasing gigs. You're creating a system that supports your creative freedom for years to come.

**What's in a Portfolio?**

A portfolio is your mix of investments. It might include:

- Stocks: high-growth, high-risk investments that can earn a lot—or lose a lot. Think of them like your boldest work: rewarding when done well, but not always predictable.
- Bonds: lower risk, lower return investments that offer more stability. These are your steady clients or grant income—less glamorous, but dependable.
- Cash: your emergency fund, your safety net. Easy to access when a show gets canceled or equipment breaks.
- Real estate, ETFs, or mutual funds: flexible options that help diversify your financial strategy.

Just like an artist works in multiple mediums or exhibits in different venues, you don't want to put all your money into one thing. That's where diversification comes in.

**Why Diversification Matters**

Putting all your money into one stock—or depending on one source of income—is risky. If that stream dries up, you're left scrambling.

Diversification is spreading your investments across different areas so your success doesn't hinge on one outcome. Just like your income might come from commissions, teaching, merch, and shows, your investments should come from multiple sources.

**Types of Portfolios – Choosing Based on Your Season**

**Conservative Portfolio**

This portfolio is mostly made up of bonds and cash, with only a small amount in stocks. It's built to protect, not to grow quickly.

This is for artists who are close to retirement, saving for a major expense, or want low risk.

Pros: Less volatility, more predictable returns

Cons: Slower growth, may not beat inflation over time

**Moderate Portfolio**

A balanced mix of stocks and bonds, this portfolio is for artists in their mid-career who want growth but don't want to take big risks.

Pros: Balance of risk and reward

Cons: May feel slow in high-growth periods

**Aggressive Portfolio**

Mostly made up of stocks and high-growth investments, this strategy is designed for building wealth long-term. It's ideal for artists in their 20s and 30s, or anyone who doesn't need to access their money for 10+ years.

Pros: Strong potential for wealth building

Cons: High volatility, emotionally tough during downturns

**Choosing Your Strategy**

Pick a more aggressive approach when:

- You're in the early stages of your career

- You don't need the money for at least 10 years
- You're okay with some ups and downs along the way

Choose a more conservative approach when:

- You need your money within a few years
- You're nearing retirement or relying on your investments
- You're risk-averse and prioritize peace of mind

**Let Your Portfolio Evolve with Your Career**

Just like your creative process changes over time, your financial strategy should shift too.

- In your 20s: Focus on growth. Take more calculated risks.
- In your 30s and 40s: Mix growth with security. Balance creative risk-taking with financial planning.
- Later in life: Shift to protection mode. You've built something worth preserving.

**Final Thoughts – Create More Than Art. Create a Legacy.**

As an artist, you already know how to create something from nothing. That same creativity, when paired with financial literacy, can build a life of freedom.

Don't chase trends. Don't get distracted by hype. Build a portfolio the same way you build your art—with discipline, vision, and time.

Your creative legacy matters. But your financial one does too. When you treat your finances like your craft, you're not just making money—you're making history.

And that's something no one can take away from you.

# Chapter 48: The Eighth Wonder of the World – Understanding Compound Interest

When people think about building wealth, most assume you need a lot of money to start. But here's the truth—wealth is built with time, not just dollars. One of the most powerful forces in finance is **compound interest**, and if you're an artist, creative, or freelancer just beginning to earn from your work, this is the best time to make it work for you.

You don't need six figures to start investing. You need consistency, a long-term mindset, and time. That's it.

**What Is Compound Interest?**

Compound interest is when your money earns interest—and then that interest earns more interest. It's exponential growth. You're not just making money on what you put in—you're making money on the money you've already made.

It's the difference between pushing a bike up a hill and suddenly coasting down it. The longer you let compound interest work, the faster and farther your money goes.

**Example:**

If you invest $1,000 at a 10% annual return:

- Year 1: You earn $100 (total = $1,100)
- Year 2: You earn $110 (total = $1,210)

- Year 3: You earn $121 (total = $1,331)

The gains keep growing without you having to do anything extra—like a creative project that keeps paying you royalties.

**Artists and Time: Why It Matters**

As an artist, you might not always know when the next big check is coming in. Your income may fluctuate. That's why **starting early** and **staying consistent** is your superpower. The earlier you begin investing—even if it's $50/month—the more time your money has to grow.

Consider two creatives:

- *Painter A* starts investing $200/month at age 22 and stops at 32
- *Dancer B* starts at 32 and keeps going until 65

Even though Painter A only invested for 10 years, their money may grow more over time than Dancer B's—just because they started earlier. That's compound interest at work.

**The Rule of 72 – Your Shortcut to Doubling**

Here's a quick trick: divide 72 by your expected annual return. That gives you an estimate of how long it'll take your money to double.

- 72 ÷ 6% = 12 years
- 72 ÷ 8% = 9 years
- 72 ÷ 10% = 7.2 years

So, if you invest $10,000 and earn 8%, you'll have $20,000 in 9 years—even without adding more. That's how you turn small wins into big freedom.

**Where Artists Can Use Compound Interest**

You don't need to be a financial pro. These accounts are easy ways to let compound interest do the heavy lifting:

- **Roth IRA** – Tax-free growth and withdrawals
- **Traditional IRA or 401(k)** – Tax-deferred growth

- **High-yield savings** – Lower returns, but still compounds
- **Brokerage accounts** – Great for flexible investing
- **SEP IRA** – Perfect if you're a self-employed creative running your own studio or business

### But Compound Interest Can Hurt Too

If you're carrying high-interest **credit card debt**, that's compound interest working against you. Artists who finance equipment or rack up expenses on cards may pay thousands in interest over time.

Let's say you owe $3,000 on a card at 20%. If you only make minimum payments, it could take years to pay off—and you'll end up spending way more than $3,000.

The same principle that builds wealth can also build debt.

**Protect Yourself:**

- Pay credit cards in full each month
- Avoid payday loans or financing unnecessary purchases
- Track your spending and stick to a plan
- Invest consistently—even small amounts matter

### Mindset Shift: Spend vs. Invest

Every dollar you spend on something temporary is a dollar that doesn't grow.

Before you hit "buy," ask yourself:

- Could this dollar be working for me?
- Will this expense still matter five years from now?
- What if I invested this in my future instead?

You don't have to live without joy—but balance is key. The same way you budget time for practice, paint, rehearsal, or edits, budget money for now *and* later.

**How to Start Using Compound Interest**

- Open a Roth IRA (if you have income)—start with a platform like Fidelity, Schwab, or Vanguard
- Contribute what you can: $50/month is better than nothing
- Choose an index fund (like S&P 500 or Total Market)
- Let it grow—don't touch it!
- Reinvest earnings
- Increase your contribution when you get a raise, land a commission, or license your work

**Final Thoughts: Your Financial Future Is a Masterpiece in Progress**

As an artist, you already understand delayed gratification. You put in hours—sometimes years—before your work pays off. Compound interest is no different.

Start small. Stay consistent. Let time do what it does best.

Because the biggest difference between artists who struggle and artists who thrive long-term? It's not talent. It's planning. It's systems. It's letting your money *do the work* while you create, live, and dream.

Let compound interest be your quiet collaborator—the one building your future while you build your craft.

# Chapter 49: Culture: The Lens That Shapes How You See Money

## Financial Literacy Begins with Your Story

Financial literacy doesn't start with a bank account or a budget app. It starts with your story—your upbringing, your influences, your community, and how money was (or wasn't) talked about in your world.

Let's keep it real: depending on your race, gender, background, and environment, you've likely developed a very specific lens through which you view money. And that lens shapes how you earn, spend, save, or avoid dealing with finances altogether.

### *Your Lens Is Unique*

If you were raised by a single parent hustling to keep the lights on, where the only conversation about money was "we don't have any," it makes sense if you feel pressure to earn as fast as possible—or feel guilt when spending on yourself.

If you grew up seeing entertainers or local artists being praised when they finally "made it," but also saw them struggle quietly behind the scenes, then money might represent freedom, validation, or escape. And if your community told you that art isn't a real job? You might carry a chip on your shoulder—or internalize the fear of failure, no matter how talented you are.

If you found out someone misused your name or identity to open credit cards or ran up bills in your name, it's no wonder if you have trust issues around banks or financial professionals.

No matter where you come from, this much is true: your experience shaped your money mindset. But that mindset doesn't have to define your future.

## You Can't Change Where You Come From—But You Can Change Where You're Going

The fact that you're reading this means you're ready to do something different. You're ready to build a creative career that's sustainable. You're ready to stop stressing about bills and start thinking about ownership, options, and building a legacy through your work.

That starts by reclaiming control over your money story.

You don't have to be a math whiz. You don't need a business degree. You don't even need to be good with numbers. What you need is a willingness to learn.

Ask your accountant questions until you understand. Make your financial advisor break things down in plain English. If you're signing a licensing deal, don't just glance at it—ask a lawyer to explain it line by line.

**Because here's the truth:** your team works for you. But if you don't understand the financial playbook, how will you know if they're running the right plays?

## Learn the Game—So You Don't Get Played

Every year, we hear stories of musicians, actors, designers, and painters who went broke—not because they weren't talented or successful—but because they didn't understand what was happening with their money. That's heartbreaking—and avoidable.

If your community didn't talk about money, it's time to break that silence.

Ask questions. Take workshops. Read books. Watch YouTube videos. Follow creators who teach finance with creatives in mind.

You don't need to know everything. But you do need to know enough to protect yourself, your work, and your future.

## This Is Bigger Than You

You might be the first in your family to earn steady income from your art. You might be the first to turn your creativity into a business. That's not a burden—that's power.

By learning how to manage your money now, you're not just building for yourself. You're creating a roadmap for the next generation of artists in your family, your studio, or your city. You're showing that it's possible to be both creative and financially strong.

## Final Word

Your background may have shaped your perspective on money—but it doesn't have to limit you.

Whether you grew up with abundance or anxiety, your financial literacy journey starts here. You deserve to understand your money. You deserve peace of mind. You deserve the freedom to make choices based on what you love—not based on fear, debt, or confusion.

Let's change the narrative that artists must struggle. Let's make room for a new generation of creatives who build not just art—but assets, security, and legacy.

Because when you understand money, you don't just survive—you thrive.

You create on your own terms.

You stop working paycheck to paycheck and start designing a life that sustains your vision.

Let's build that together.

# Chapter 50: Your Network Is Your Studio Crew – Build Relationships That Outlast the Applause

When the curtain closes, the last flash fades, or the final track drops, one thing becomes clear: talent may open the first door, but relationships are what keep doors opening.

Every artist needs a network—a team offstage, off-camera, or outside the gallery that helps you grow your career, navigate opportunities, and stay grounded. Think of them like your behind-the-scenes crew: collaborators, mentors, agents, managers, accountants, former professors, gallery owners, and supporters who believe in your vision and want to help you succeed.

Whether you're painting, performing, producing, or building a brand—your art needs an ecosystem.

## *Why Relationships Matter More Than Algorithms*

Let's be real: it's tempting to focus on followers and likes. Social media can feel like the end-all-be-all for exposure. But a viral post doesn't pay the bills consistently—and a million followers won't help you read a contract, file your taxes, or negotiate licensing terms.

Here's the truth:

**Fans clap. Relationships build.**

Your network can help you:

- Land your first gallery showing
- Get connected with agencies or production houses
- Book festivals, commissions, or tours
- Collaborate with trusted creatives
- Learn how to price and protect your work
- Get referred to a financial advisor, lawyer, or accountant who "gets" artists

## *Your Art Is Personal—So Should Be Your Network*

Start with who you already know:

- **Art school peers** – They're growing too. Stay connected.
- **Former professors or instructors** – They can open doors you didn't even know existed.
- **Fellow artists and collaborators** – Don't treat them like competition. Build each other up.
- **Brand reps or gallery managers** you've worked with – Stay in touch. Send updates. Ask how you can support *them*, too.

Relationships deepen when you reach out *without asking for anything*—when you simply connect, offer support, or show appreciation.

Example message:

"Hey [Name], I just wanted to say thank you for the opportunity to show work at your gallery last year. I'd love to hear more about what you're working on and how I can stay involved in the future."

## *Build a Team Behind the Canvas*

In sports, it's common to have a coach, trainer, and nutritionist. As an artist, you need your own version of that:

- **Mentors** – Artists or entrepreneurs who are 5–10 years ahead of you.

- **Peers** – Creatives who are in the grind with you and can keep you motivated.
- **Industry pros** – Accountants, business attorneys, or agents who specialize in creative work.

These are the people who can:

- Explain royalty agreements or contract clauses
- Keep you on track with quarterly taxes
- Help you build a brand, not just a body of work
- Protect your rights while expanding your reach

And yes—this takes effort. But so does your craft. So does your vision. And the right people around you will help make both sustainable.

### *Real Networking Isn't Transactional*

You don't need a slick elevator pitch or a perfectly curated feed to build genuine connections. You just need to:

- Show up with curiosity
- Follow through on what you say you'll do
- Give value before asking for help
- Stay in touch—even when you don't "need" something

It's not about collecting contacts. It's about cultivating community.

### *Don't Just Chase Fans—Build a Creative Family*

Let's break it down.

**Fans**

- Double-tap your post

- Celebrate your wins
- Might buy your art or ticket once

**Relationships**

- Introduce you to new collectors or venues
- Help you negotiate better deals
- Encourage you when you're stuck creatively
- Show up for you when no one's watching

A hundred strong relationships will get you further than a hundred thousand empty followers.

## *How to Start Building Today*

- **Reconnect with 5 people** who've supported your art or career
- **Send a thank-you message** to someone who inspired or booked you
- **Reach out to one mentor** or professional you admire—ask if they'd hop on a quick call
- **Support other artists** — share their work, buy their zines, show up at their openings

Because the more you give, the more you grow.

## *Final Word: Build Your Offstage Crew*

Behind every great artist is a circle of people who believed before the world did. Build that circle intentionally.

Because when the show ends, and the trends shift, and the clicks slow down—your relationships are what remain. Your reputation, your support system, your creative crew.

Don't just focus on exposure.

Focus on connection.

Don't just build your audience.

Build your team.

Because one day, when you're negotiating your next big commission or licensing your work for a major brand, it won't be a follower who helps you do it—it'll be someone who knows your name, your value, and your worth.

And you'll be glad you built your network as intentionally as you built your art.

# Chapter 51: Conclusion: Art + Money = Freedom

You've made it to the end of this book, but this is just the beginning of your financial journey as an artist.

Let's be real—choosing to live a creative life takes courage. It's not easy to put your heart into your work, expose your soul to the world, and still try to figure out how to keep the lights on, how to afford a studio, how to pay off debt, how to buy time so you can create. But here's what's true: the more you understand about money, the more control you'll have over your art, your life, and your future.

Throughout these chapters, you've learned:

- How to build a budget—even when your income is inconsistent
- Why separating business and personal finances is essential
- How to track income, manage taxes, and plan for retirement
- How to price your work, protect your rights, and build multiple income streams
- And most importantly, how to *think like a creative entrepreneur* without sacrificing your passion or your integrity

Financial literacy is not about becoming obsessed with money. It's about clarity. Confidence. Peace of mind. It's knowing that you can take a month off without spiraling. It's having the freedom to walk away from a bad deal. It's charging your worth without apologizing. It's understanding the contract before you sign it. It's knowing where your money is going, how to make it grow, and how to make it last.

If you've felt shame, fear, confusion, or overwhelm when it comes to money—you're not alone. And you're not behind. What matters is that you've taken the time to learn. To shift your mindset. To ask questions. To seek answers. That's what growth looks like.

And if you've ever felt like being an artist meant you had to struggle financially, I hope this book helped you see a different path. Because you don't have to choose between creating art and creating wealth.

You can do both.

So keep going. Keep learning. Keep building. And above all—keep creating.

Your art is your voice. Your money is your power. Use both to build the life you were meant to live.

—Pat Brown, MBA

# About the Author

**Pat Brown, MBA** is a former Division I football player turned financial educator, advisor, and passionate advocate for financial literacy—especially among young creatives, student-athletes, and underrepresented communities. With a unique background that blends high-level athletics, real-world financial expertise, and a deep understanding of cultural dynamics, Pat has made it his mission to help others take control of their financial lives.

After serving as a team captain at the University of Kansas and briefly playing professionally in the CFL, Pat transitioned into financial services, earning his MBA and spending over two decades helping individuals and families build wealth. His journey into financial literacy was personal: witnessing financial struggles in his own family and among teammates lit a fire in him to educate and empower others—especially those who often get left out of traditional financial conversations.

Pat is the founder of **FinancialLiteracyForNIL.com**, a groundbreaking platform created to educate student-athletes on budgeting, credit, investing, NIL income, and building long-term wealth. He also created companion platforms like *Financial Literacy for the Culture*, *Financial Literacy for Student-Athletes*, *Financial Literacy for College Coaches*, and *Financial Literacy for Artists*, all designed to speak to specific audiences with relevant, actionable insights.

This book is especially personal. Pat's daughter, Ryan "Madison" Brown, is a graduate of the Fashion Institute of Technology (F.I.T.) and a talented young artist. Their ongoing conversations about money, contracts, credit, and independence inspired him to create a resource for creatives like her—artists, designers, dancers, writers, and more—who need real-world financial knowledge as they pursue their passions.

Whether you're building a brand, freelancing full-time, or simply want to make smarter money moves as an artist, Pat's work will help you see that you're not just creating art—you're building a future. The game might end, the project might ship, the gallery might close—but financial literacy is the legacy that keeps creating.

# Disclaimer and Educational Purpose

This book, *Financial Literacy for Artists,* was written to educate, empower, and inspire creatives—whether you're a painter, designer, filmmaker, dancer, photographer, actor, musician, or multi-hyphenate—to take ownership of your financial future. The guidance throughout this book is based on the author's personal experience as a financial professional and as a parent of an artist, as well as decades of research and real-world observations across both the creative and financial industries.

That said, please understand the following:

## *This Book Does Not Provide Legal, Tax, or Financial Advice*

The contents of this book are for general educational and informational purposes only. This is not a substitute for personalized advice from qualified professionals. Every artist's situation is different. Your income streams, tax liabilities, contract terms, business structure, and career goals may vary significantly from the examples in this book.

Before making any financial, legal, or business decisions—including but not limited to:

- Signing contracts
- Filing taxes
- Starting a business
- Investing your money
- Applying for grants or loans
- Licensing your intellectual property
- **you should consult with a licensed professional.** That includes a

financial advisor, CPA, business manager, lawyer, or tax expert who understands the unique challenges and nuances of working in the creative space.

### *No Legal Advice*

Contracts are a core part of the creative industry—from licensing and performance agreements to commissions and distribution deals. This book may refer to those topics in general terms, but it does **not** provide legal advice or replace the guidance of an attorney. If you're unsure about your rights, ownership, or obligations under a contract, please consult a legal professional before signing.

### *No Guarantees of Financial Outcomes*

The strategies, case studies, and rules of thumb in this book are based on general principles and educational intent. They are **not** guarantees of financial success. Artists face unique market conditions, variable income, and industry-specific pressures that affect financial outcomes. This book is here to provide you with a toolkit—not a one-size-fits-all formula.

### *Always Do Your Own Research*

Tax laws, grant requirements, business license regulations, and platform policies change frequently. Artists who earn income through multiple sources—freelance work, streaming royalties, print sales, performances, or brand deals—need to stay informed. Use this book as a starting point, but always cross-check information and confirm with a trusted professional or up-to-date resource.

## *Liability Disclaimer*

The author, Pat Brown, MBA, and associated platforms (including *FinancialLiteracyForArtists.com*, *FinancialLiteracyForNIL.com*, and others) disclaim all liability for actions taken or not taken based on the contents of this book. Readers assume full responsibility for any choices they make regarding their personal finances, business operations, or legal decisions.

## *Encouragement to Build a Support Team*

Every artist deserves a trusted team. A good accountant, an honest attorney, a knowledgeable financial advisor, and a solid circle of fellow creatives can help you grow while avoiding costly mistakes. If you don't yet have a financial support system—start building one. It's one of the best investments you'll ever make.

# Financial Literacy Calendar for Artists: Key Dates & Deadlines

**JANUARY**

- Jan 1: New Tax Year Begins
- Start tracking all income and expenses
- Set aside 25–30% of income for taxes
- Open a business checking account (if you haven't already)
- Jan 15: 4th Quarter Estimated Tax Payment Due
- File IRS Form 1040-ES if you earned $1,000+ last year without tax withholding
- Jan 31: Deadline for Receiving Tax Forms
- Form 1099-NEC (endorsement/sponsor income)
- Form 1099-K (platform payments over $600)
- W-2 (if employed by an organization)

**FEBRUARY**

- Begin organizing tax paperwork
- Collect receipts, mileage logs, gear expenses, and all income forms
- Prepare to file:
- Schedule C (self-employed income)
- Schedule SE (self-employment tax)

**MARCH**

- Mar 15: Tax Filing Deadline for S-Corps/LLCs (with election)
- File Form 1120S if applicable

**APRIL**

- Apr 15: Federal Income Tax Filing Deadline
- File Form 1040
- File Form 4868 for an extension if needed
- Make 1st Quarter Estimated Tax Payment
- Last day to contribute to prior year's IRA or HSA

**MAY**

- Review financial goals & tax outcome
- Adjust savings plan and estimated tax strategy if needed

**JUNE**

- Jun 15: 2nd Quarter Estimated Tax Payment Due
- Revisit income tracking and adjust set-asides for tax obligations

**JULY**

- Jul 1: Mid-Year Review
- Reassess contracts, rates, retirement savings, and expenses
- Consider forming an LLC if income is steady and increasing

**AUGUST**

- Prep for fall income and expenses
- Begin prepping for year-end financial goals

**SEPTEMBER**

- Sep 15: 3rd Quarter Estimated Tax Payment Due
- Audit expense tracking and begin organizing for tax season

**OCTOBER**

- Oct 1: FAFSA Opens (if you're a student or dependent)
- Oct 15: Final Deadline to Submit Extended Tax Returns

**NOVEMBER**

- Year-End Planning Begins
- Book a meeting with a CPA or financial advisor
- Buy deductible business expenses (gear, services, etc.)
- Make charitable contributions

**DECEMBER**

- Dec 31: Last Day to Complete Key Tax Moves
- Business expenses, SEP IRA, Solo 401(k) contributions
- Final chance to close NIL deals for the year

**BONUS BEST PRACTICES**

- Save 25% to 30% of all income for taxes
- Separate personal and business finances
- Log all expenses, miles, and payments
- Use digital tools: QuickBooks, Keeper Tax, MileIQ
- Work with pros: tax preparers, CPAs, and financial advisors
- Check your state tax laws regularly

**Tip:** Even if you're just getting started, consistency is key. A well-kept calendar and monthly review habit can save you thousands in taxes and missed opportunities.

# Questions for Financial Advisors, CPA's, Attoneys

**Questions for a Financial Advisor**

1. How do I start investing with irregular income?
2. What percentage of my income should I save or invest?
3. Should I open a Roth IRA or a Traditional IRA?
4. How much should I contribute to retirement if I'm self-employed?
5. How can I prepare for retirement without a 401(k)?
6. How much should I keep in my emergency fund?
7. What are the best budgeting strategies for freelancers?
8. Can you help me create a financial plan for the next 5 to 10 years?
9. What should my financial priorities be if I'm just starting out?
10. Should I pay off debt or invest first?
11. How can I build wealth over time with small contributions?
12. What is the best way to track my net worth?
13. How do I manage large, inconsistent payments?
14. How can I avoid lifestyle creep during successful years?
15. What's the right asset allocation for someone with fluctuating income?
16. Should I invest in real estate or stay in more liquid assets?
17. How do I choose between index funds, mutual funds, and individual stocks?
18. How do I know if I need disability or liability insurance?
19. Should I invest in my art business or in traditional assets first?
20. How do I set income goals that align with financial independence?

## Questions for a CPA or Tax Professional

1. Do I need to pay quarterly estimated taxes?
2. What forms do I need to file as a freelance artist?
3. What tax deductions can I take as an artist?
4. Can I deduct art supplies, materials, and equipment?
5. Can I write off my home studio?
6. Can I deduct travel expenses related to shows or exhibitions?
7. How do I report income from Etsy, Shopify, or other platforms?
8. What are the tax implications of receiving grant money?
9. Is prize money from contests taxable?
10. What happens if I don't file quarterly estimated taxes?
11. Can I deduct education or training related to my craft?
12. What's the best way to keep track of my expenses?
13. Should I use software or hire a bookkeeper?
14. Should I separate my business and personal finances?
15. Can I write off health insurance if I'm self-employed?
16. Am I allowed to deduct meals or entertainment for client meetings?
17. Are commissions paid to other artists or collaborators deductible?
18. Do I need to issue 1099s to assistants or contractors?
19. When do I cross the line from a hobby to a business in the IRS's eyes?
20. What records should I keep to protect myself in an audit?

## Questions for a Business Attorney

1. Should I form an LLC, S-Corp, or remain a sole proprietor?
2. What are the benefits of having an LLC as an artist?
3. How do I protect my intellectual property?
4. Should I copyright my artwork?
5. Do I need a trademark for my logo or artist name?
6. How can I license my work to brands or companies?
7. What should I include in a commission agreement?
8. What do I do if someone uses my artwork without permission?

9. Can I sue someone for using my art without credit?
10. What rights do I keep when selling original art?
11. What is the difference between usage rights and ownership?
12. Should I use a contract for every sale or commission?
13. What happens if a client doesn't pay me for work?
14. What's the legal process to collect unpaid invoices?
15. How do I protect myself when collaborating with other artists?
16. Should I consult an attorney before signing a gallery or licensing agreement?
17. What legal documents do I need to sell work online?
18. Should I include terms and conditions on my website?
19. Can I use testimonials and client work in my portfolio legally?
20. What are my responsibilities if I start hiring assistants?

**Questions for Insurance Professionals**

1. Do I need business liability insurance?
2. What is errors and omissions insurance, and do I need it?
3. Is my artwork covered if it's stolen or damaged in transit?
4. Do I need renter's insurance if I store work at home?
5. Should I insure my studio space separately?
6. What kind of health insurance is best for self-employed artists?
7. Is disability insurance worth it if I rely on my hands for my art?
8. What happens if I get hurt and can't work?
9. Should I get equipment insurance for my camera, laptop, or tools?
10. How do I make sure my insurance covers art I sell internationally?

**Questions for Retirement Account or Wealth Professionals**

1. How do I open a Solo 401(k) or SEP IRA?
2. Which is better for me: SEP IRA, SIMPLE IRA, or Roth IRA?
3. How much can I contribute annually to each type of account?
4. Can I still contribute to retirement if I don't have consistent income?

5. Are there tax breaks for contributing to a retirement account?
6. Can I invest my retirement money in socially responsible funds?
7. What's the penalty if I withdraw money early from an IRA?
8. What are my options if I want to retire early?
9. How do I automate retirement contributions from my art income?
10. What happens to my retirement accounts if I die without a will?

## Questions About General Business Strategy

1. How do I price my work for profitability?
2. What's the best way to calculate my hourly rate?
3. Should I charge a flat fee or hourly for custom work?
4. How do I build a sustainable income with multiple revenue streams?
5. When should I start thinking about hiring help?
6. What's the best business bank account or credit card for artists?
7. How do I track inventory for my products?
8. Should I get a resale certificate for buying materials tax-free?
9. What financial reports should I review monthly or quarterly?
10. Should I use accounting software like QuickBooks or Wave?
11. Can I deduct startup costs for launching a new product line?
12. How should I handle sales tax in different states or countries?
13. What is nexus and how does it affect my online sales?
14. What are the financial risks of doing business internationally?
15. How do I prepare for slower months in my business?
16. What's the best way to reinvest profits into my business?
17. Should I open a business savings account?
18. What financial metrics should I track as a creative entrepreneur?
19. What should I do if I'm behind on taxes or in debt?
20. What's one thing you think every artist overlooks financially?

# Definitions

**1. Asset**

Anything of value that you own, such as cash, investments, property, or equipment.

**2. Liability**

A financial obligation or debt owed to another party.

**3. Net Worth**

Your total assets minus your total liabilities.

**4. Income**

Money received from work, sales, investments, or other sources.

**5. Expense**

Money spent on goods or services, including business and personal costs.

**6. Profit**

The amount of income left over after subtracting expenses from revenue.

**7. Loss**

Occurs when expenses exceed income or revenue in a given period.

**8. Budget**

A plan that outlines expected income and expenses over a period of time.

**9. Cash Flow**

The total amount of money being transferred in and out of your accounts.

**10. Gross Income**

The total income earned before taxes and deductions.

**11. Net Income**

Income remaining after taxes and deductions—also called "take-home pay."

**12. Self-Employment Income**

Money earned from running your own business or freelancing.

**13. W-2**

A tax form showing income earned and taxes withheld from employment.

**14. 1099-NEC**

A tax form for reporting payments made to self-employed individuals or contractors.

**15. 1099-K**

A tax form issued by payment processors if you received more than $600 via apps like Venmo or PayPal.

**16. Schedule C**

A tax form used by self-employed individuals to report business income and expenses.

**17. Schedule SE**

A form used to calculate self-employment taxes.

**18. IRS Form 1040**

The main individual income tax return form filed annually.

**19. Form 1040-ES**

Used to calculate and pay estimated quarterly taxes.

**20. Estimated Taxes**

Quarterly tax payments made by self-employed people who don't have taxes withheld.

**21. Business Entity**

A legally recognized business structure, such as an LLC, S-Corp, or sole proprietorship.

**22. LLC (Limited Liability Company)**

A business structure that protects personal assets from business debts or lawsuits.

**23. S-Corp**

A type of corporation that passes income through to shareholders to avoid double taxation.

**24. Sole Proprietorship**

A simple business structure with one owner, no legal distinction between owner and business.

**25. EIN (Employer Identification Number)**

A unique ID number issued by the IRS for businesses, used for tax filing and opening bank accounts.

**26. Bookkeeping**

The process of recording financial transactions.

**27. Accounting**

The process of summarizing, analyzing, and reporting financial information.

**28. Accounts Receivable**

Money owed to you by clients or customers for services rendered.

**29. Accounts Payable**

Money you owe to vendors or others for goods and services.

**30. Invoice**

A document requesting payment for goods or services provided.

**31. Receipt**

A document confirming payment received.

**32. Tax Deduction**

An expense that can be subtracted from taxable income to reduce tax liability.

**33. Tax Credit**

A direct reduction of your tax bill, dollar-for-dollar.

**34. Depreciation**

The reduction in value of an asset over time due to wear and tear or usage.

**35. Capital Gains**

Profits from the sale of investments or assets.

**36. Capital Losses**

Losses incurred from the sale of investments or assets for less than their original cost.

**37. Diversification**

Spreading investments across different assets to reduce risk.

**38. Risk Tolerance**

Your comfort level with potential losses in your investment portfolio.

**39. Investment Portfolio**

A collection of financial assets such as stocks, bonds, and mutual funds.

**40. Stock**

A share of ownership in a publicly traded company.

**41. Bond**

A debt instrument where you lend money to a company or government in exchange for interest.

**42. ETF (Exchange-Traded Fund)**

A fund that owns multiple assets and trades like a stock on exchanges.

**43. Mutual Fund**

A professionally managed investment fund made up of pooled money from many investors.

**44. Dividend**

A portion of a company's earnings distributed to shareholders.

**45. IRA (Individual Retirement Account)**

A retirement savings account with tax benefits.

**46. Roth IRA**

A type of IRA where contributions are made with after-tax money and withdrawals are tax-free in retirement.

**47. SEP IRA**

A retirement account designed for self-employed individuals and small business owners.

**48. Solo 401(k)**

A retirement plan for self-employed people with no employees.

**49. Emergency Fund**

Savings set aside for unexpected expenses or emergencies.

**50. Credit Score**

A number representing your creditworthiness, used by lenders.

**51. Credit Report**

A detailed record of your borrowing and repayment history.

**52. APR (Annual Percentage Rate)**

The cost of borrowing money on a yearly basis, expressed as a percentage.

**53. Compound Interest**

Interest earned on both the principal and accumulated interest.

**54. Simple Interest**

Interest earned only on the principal amount.

**55. Principal**

The original amount of money invested or loaned.

**56. Retirement Account Contribution Limit**

The maximum amount you can contribute to retirement accounts in a year.

**57. Business Expense**

An ordinary and necessary cost for running a business.

**58. Fixed Expense**

A recurring cost that doesn't change month to month (e.g., rent).

**59. Variable Expense**

A cost that changes depending on usage (e.g., travel, supplies).

**60. Royalties**

Income earned from intellectual property, like books, music, or art licensing.

**61. Licensing**

Allowing another party to use your creative work in exchange for a fee or royalty.

**62. Copyright**

A legal protection for original creative works.

**63. Trademark**

A legal protection for logos, names, or symbols that represent a brand.

**64. Intellectual Property (IP)**

Creations of the mind—art, inventions, writing—protected by law.

**65. Artist Grant**

Funding provided to artists by institutions or nonprofits, usually for specific projects.

**66. Commission**

A custom project or work of art ordered and paid for by a client.

**67. Retainer**

A fee paid in advance to secure services over a period of time.

**68. Fiscal Sponsor**

A nonprofit that allows artists to receive tax-deductible donations for their projects.

**69. Crowdfunding**

Raising money from a large number of people, often through platforms like Kickstarter or GoFundMe.

**70. Business Insurance**

Insurance coverage that protects against risks like liability or property loss.

**71. Professional Liability Insurance**

Coverage for claims of negligence or harm resulting from your work.

**72. Deductible (Insurance)**

The amount you pay out of pocket before insurance covers the rest.

**73. Audit**

An examination of your financial records by the IRS or a CPA.

**74. Financial Plan**

A roadmap for your money—includes goals, savings, debt, and investment strategies.

**75. Passive Income**

Earnings from investments or royalties that require little active effort.

**76. Active Income**

Earnings from direct work, like painting, teaching, or consulting.

**77. Freelancer**

A self-employed person offering services to multiple clients.

**78. Contractor**

A non-employee who performs work for a business under a contract.

**79. Retained Earnings**

The portion of net income not distributed as dividends but reinvested in the business.

**80. Break-Even Point**

When your revenue equals your expenses—no profit, no loss.

**81. Grant Proposal**

A written request for funding submitted to a grant-making institution.

**82. Fiscal Year**

A 12-month period used for accounting and tax purposes, not always aligned with the calendar year.

**83. Taxable Income**

Income on which you must pay taxes, after deductions.

**84. Adjusted Gross Income (AGI)**

Your gross income minus specific deductions (like student loan interest).

**85. Tax Bracket**

A range of incomes taxed at a specific rate.

**86. Safe Harbor Rule**

A tax guideline that protects you from penalties if you meet specific payment thresholds.

**87. Mileage Log**

A record of miles driven for business purposes—can be deductible.

**88. Per Diem**

A daily allowance for expenses like food and lodging when traveling for work.

**89. Fair Market Value**

The price something would sell for on the open market.

**90. Depreciable Asset**

A long-term asset whose cost is spread out over its useful life.

**91. Chart of Accounts**

A list of all accounts used in your bookkeeping system.

**92. General Ledger**

The master record of all your financial transactions.

**93. Trial Balance**

A report that ensures all credits and debits are equal in your accounts.

**94. Balance Sheet**

A snapshot of your financial position: assets, liabilities, and equity at a point in time.

**95. Income Statement**

A report showing your income and expenses over a specific period—also called a profit & loss statement.

**96. Cash Basis Accounting**

Recording income and expenses only when money changes hands.

**97. Accrual Basis Accounting**

Recording income and expenses when they're incurred, regardless of payment date.

**98. Financial Statement**

A summary of your business's financial performance and position.

**99. Payroll Taxes**

Taxes you must pay if you hire employees—including Social Security, Medicare, and unemployment.

**100. Withholding**

The portion of income held back by an employer (or self-employed individual) to cover taxes.

# Essential Tax Forms for Independent Artists

**1. IRS Form 1040 – U.S. Individual Income Tax Return**

- This is your **main federal tax form**.
- You'll use this form to report all income—freelance, W-2, investments, and more.
- You'll attach additional forms like Schedule C, SE, and others depending on your situation.
- **Due Date:** April 15 (or the next business day if it falls on a weekend/holiday).

**2. Schedule C (Form 1040) – Profit or Loss From Business**

- This is where **you report all your self-employment income and expenses** as a creative entrepreneur.
- You list your business income (what you were paid) and subtract your business expenses (materials, equipment, software, travel, etc.) to calculate profit or loss.
- If you operate under your own name without forming an LLC or other business entity, you're a **sole proprietor**, and this is the form you'll use.

**3. Schedule SE (Form 1040) – Self-Employment Tax**

- This calculates your **Social Security and Medicare tax** as someone who is self-employed.

- As an independent artist, you are both the employer and employee, so you owe both halves.
- The current self-employment tax rate is **15.3%** (12.4% for Social Security, 2.9% for Medicare).
- Based on your net profit from Schedule C.

**4. Form 1099-NEC – Nonemployee Compensation**

- If a brand, company, or client pays you **$600 or more** for services in a year, they are supposed to send you this form.
- **You do not fill this out**, but you must report the income from it.
- If you didn't receive one but earned money, you must still report the income on Schedule C.

**5. Form 1099-K – Payment Card and Third-Party Network Transactions**

- You may receive this if you **collected over $600** in payments through platforms like **PayPal, Venmo, Square, or Etsy**.
- **Important:** Even if you don't receive a 1099-K, you must still report all income.

**6. Form W-9 – Request for Taxpayer Identification Number**

- You'll fill this out when a client or company requests your **legal name, address, and Social Security Number (or EIN)** so they can issue you a 1099.
- You usually fill this out **before you are paid**.

**7. Form 8829 – Expenses for Business Use of Your Home**

- If you use part of your home **exclusively** for your art or creative business (a studio, office, etc.), you can deduct part of your rent, utilities, and internet.

- This form calculates that home office deduction.

**8. Form 4562 – Depreciation and Amortization**

- Use this if you buy **expensive equipment** (camera, kiln, printing press, etc.) that you want to **depreciate over several years** instead of writing off all at once.
- Often used when equipment costs **more than $2,500**.

**9. Form 1040-ES – Estimated Tax Payments**

- If you expect to owe **$1,000 or more in taxes** from freelance/self-employment work, the IRS wants you to make **quarterly estimated payments**.
- Form 1040-ES is used to calculate and send in those payments.
- **Due Dates:**
- Q1: April 15
- Q2: June 15
- Q3: September 15
- Q4: January 15 (of the following year)

**10. Form W-2 – Wage and Tax Statement**

- You'll receive this **if you worked a part-time or full-time job as an employee**, even if your main income was freelance art.
- Include this income on your Form 1040.

**11. Form 4868 – Application for Automatic Extension of Time to File U.S. Income Tax Return**

- Use this if you need more time to gather forms and file.

- **Note:** This is only an extension to file—not to pay.
- You still need to **estimate and pay taxes by April 15** to avoid penalties.

## *Optional or Specialized Forms*

### 12. Form 1098-T – Tuition Statement

- If you took art classes or continuing education, you might receive this from your school.
- May qualify you for education tax credits.

### 13. Form 8880 – Retirement Savings Contributions Credit

- If you contributed to a **Roth IRA, Traditional IRA, or Solo 401(k)** and your income is under certain limits, you may qualify for a tax credit.

### 14. Form 5329 – Additional Taxes on Qualified Plans (Including IRAs)

- If you took money out of a retirement account early or didn't take required distributions, you may need to use this form.

### 15. Form 8962 – Premium Tax Credit

- If you received health insurance through the Marketplace and used subsidies, you'll need this to reconcile the amount received.

## *Key Takeaways for Artists*

- **Track all income and expenses** year-round using spreadsheets or apps like QuickBooks, Wave, or Keeper Tax.
- Keep **receipts, invoices, mileage logs**, and separate your **personal and business accounts**.
- If you're earning consistently, consider forming an **LLC or getting an**

**EIN** for better protection and structure.

- **Hire a tax professional** if you're unsure how to handle deductions, depreciation, or estimated payments.

Made in the USA
Monee, IL
04 November 2026

67386740R00193